Advance Praise for Spirit Script

A Down-to-Earth Guide to the Things of Heaven

"Your reflections are both spiritually provocative and practically helpful. Many will find your book a down-to-earth guide to heaven."

—*Francis Cardinal George, O.M.I.*

Francis Cardinal George, O.M.I., Archbishop of Chicago

A Prayer for the 21st Century

"Regine Fanning has written a book that should be a staple in the library of anyone seeking to slow down and tap into the sacred in the everyday. She uses the Psalms as a springboard for prayer, knowing full well that these ancient texts also contain more action, more drama, and more plot twists than the latest movie. She knows fully well that the Psalms are the Rosetta Stone to understanding the human condition. And when we understand ourselves, we can lead a more contemplative, and, therefore, more meaningful, life. This is wisdom offered in bite sizes that can be savored at an airport, riding a commuter train, or sitting at home in a comfortable chair with a candle and incense burning. It is prayer for the toll collector and the computer analyst, the homemaker and the securities trader, the seeker and the already devout. It is prayer for the 21st century.

—*Judith Valente*

Judith Valente is a journalist, poet, and essayist. She is an on-air correspondent for "Religion & Ethics NewsWeekly" on PBS-TV, the author of the anthology "Twenty Poems to Nourish Your Soul" and two collections of poetry.

Engaging in a Simple, Yet Profound Way

"Regine's *Spirit Script: Praying with the Psalms* is a lovely, poetic, gentle text that is highly readable and engaging in a simple, yet profound way. She certainly wrote for a general audience and the accessible language is highly an invitation to anyone interested in pausing with the Psalms and discovering how God writes on our human hearts. I was reminded of the powerful phrase about the deep truths of faith: ancient, ever new.

In a gentle, poetic flow, each motif in *Spirit Script* is a unique threshold to the ancient treasure trove of the Psalms. Sister Regine's simple elegance of method provides readers of all ages a user-friendly access to the mystery of encounter with holiness in the everyday."

—*Avis Clendenen*

Avis Clendenen is the author of Experiencing Hildegard *and coauthor with Sister Irene Dugan, r.c. of* Love is All Around in Disguise: Mediations for Spiritual Seekers. *Currently, she is Professor of Religious Studies and Pastoral Ministry Institute Director at Saint Xavier University, Chicago.*

Aid to Any Adult's Prayer Life

"I found the work to be delightful and inspirational. While meant for the homebound, it really would serve as a fine meditative guide and aid to any adult's prayer life. A mixture of scripture resources, reflections, and poetry, it lifts mind and spirit in prayer and praise. Wisely mixing prayer, reflection, and action, it leads one ever deeper to an encounter with God. It appeals to a busy person, to "Come and see, and rest awhile," while directing them back to their real and active world. I happily and highly recommend Spirit Script to anyone seeking to expand and deepen their prayer life, or to spark their life of prayer back to life again."

—*Rev William T. Corcoran, Ph.D*

Rev William T. Corcoran, Ph.D. is Pastor, St. Linus Parish, Oak Lawn, Illinois, Dean of Deanery "D", Vicariate "V", Archdiocese of Chicago

Substance

"In an age that is addicted to superficiality, Sister Regine offers us substance. In our world, where faster is better, she invites us into the quiet places in our souls where God dwells. In a culture that craves excitement, this gifted teacher takes us into that quiet, still place within us where we learn to listen to the voice of God. I highly recommend this little book to all who are seeking a more intimate relationship with the Holy Spirit."

—*Michael J Sparough, SJ*

Michael J. Sparough latest book is What's Your Decision? *co-authored with Fr. Tim Hipskind, SJ and Jim Manney. He is Founder of Charis Ministries, Jesuit outreach to young adults in their twenties and thirties and Fountain Square Fools, a religious performing arts troupe.*

Refreshing and Delightful

"Refreshing and delightful! Poignant and to the point! With few words and a lifetime of experience, the author takes you on a journey through ordinary life with carefully selected psalms as stopping places along the way. Originally written for the homebound, *Spirit Script* carries a message for us all—there are treasures in our midst, and the age-old wisdom of the psalms is one of them!"

—*Mary Ruth Broz, RSM*

Mary Ruth Broz, RSM is on the Staff of Portiuncula Retreat Center in Frankfort, Illinois. She co-authored the book, Midwives of an Unnamed Future: A Spirituality for Women in Times of Unprecedented Change.

SPIRIT SCRIPT:

Praying With the Psalms

R E G I N E F A N N I N G , R S M

Cathedral
Rose
Books

Copyright © 2015 by Regine Fanning, RSM. All rights reserved.

No part of this publication may be reproduced, stored in a retrieval system or transmitted in any way by any means, electronic, mechanical, photocopy, recording or otherwise without the prior permission of the author except as provided by USA copyright law.

No portion of this book may be reproduced mechanically, electronically, or by any other means, including photocopying, without written permission of the publisher. It is illegal to copy this book, post it on a website, or distribute it by any other means without permission from the publisher.

Bible Verses from The New American Bible

Cathedral
Rose
Books

An Imprint of Love Your Life Publishing
427 N Tatnall Street, #90946
Wilmington, DE

636-922-2634

ISBN: 978-1-934509-87-6
Library of Congress Control Number: 2015935057
Printed in the United States of America
First Printing 2015

Author's Note

To name the "I Am."
To dream the impossible dream!

As surely as you try to name our God, so do I. Two of my favorite names are: "The God of Surprises" and "Extravagant God."

There have been many instances in my life that make both names believable. This book is the latest.

Spirit Script began in 1994. My original intent was a newsletter as a way of companioning for the homebound, one on one, monthly by mail.

Because of a promotion in the magazine *Praying*, *Spirit Script* grew, reaching readers in twenty-five states. With the final edition in December 2005, *Spirit Script* had a circulation of 500 and included the homebound, hospitals, parishes and others—like you.

My decision to conclude *Spirit Script* came after much prayer to the Holy Spirit. I was at peace with its conclusion. However, the "God of Surprises," through the inspiration and ingenuity of Alyce Christensen and

Eileen McGuire, proposed a way to continue *Spirit Script*. The result is this copy.

The blessings embracing this *Spirit Script* project are apparent. It is truly an impossible dream become a reality. Thanks to Alyce and Eileen, and their generosity of spirit, time and talent, we present to you a new edition of *Spirit Script*. A special thanks to Daniel Trompeter, who typed fourteen years of *Spirit Script* material, forging the way for this book.

Blessings for Life in the Spirit!

—Regine Fanning, RSM

Contents

I. **Getting to Know You, God** 11
   Know the God who created you.

II. **God Moments** 55
   Discover how the Spirit energizes us in unbelievable ways.

III. **Heart Work** 103
   Create a new heart, a new spirit within you: God's promise.

IV. **Interior Remodeling** 141
   Look deeper into who you are.

V. **A Nothing Day** 169
   Turn "nothing" into a shimmering day with God.

VI. **Soul Music** 211
   Sing: To sing is to pray twice.

VII. **'Tis the Season** 251
   Discover Jesus throughout the Church's liturgical seasons.

VIII. End Notes 281
Discover Jesus throughout the Church's liturgical seasons.

IX. About the Author 287

Getting to Know You, God

Introduction

Most of us learned God's name at the knees of our parents. Then, some awesome, some doubtful, and even some scary ideas about God evolved as we grew up and began to question authority.

St. Augustine concluded rightly, "Our hearts were made for God and will be restless until they rest in God."

Because ours is a living, creative God, new every morning, new every moment, the restlessness turns out to be a wonderful gift. For me, that gift opened a broader vision, a new understanding of God, the world, others, and even myself.

As children, we learned that God made the world. I believe that statement needs updating as we come to know the living God as infinite, creative, extravagant Love.

Within our universe, there is a certain dynamism that even today continues to reveal more. The new creation story is on a different page. Reading, believing, and living the present story brings us to a God-relationship that is relevant, alive, and more inclusive.

It is true that the Hebrew psalms present believers with a judging God, and that way of knowing projects fear, anger, and guilt, with heavy emphasis on sin. You can probably identify with that negative image. For instance, as a child, what did you understand your parents meant when they reminded you to be a "good" boy or girl?

In trying to live up to that "good" behavior, you were deprived of the joy that comes with the embracing presence of Love.

The Hebrew psalms voice some reality, but it is a reality of another age. Confiding their needs and anxieties in prayer to the Almighty God was a start. Oh, but what possibilities are ours!

To really pray the psalms, we have to re-image God, risk, go wild, lean into the I AM—Love beyond all telling.

While our God is Love beyond all imagining, yet our relationship can continue to grow and deepen. In fact, that is God's intent. That intent is not new, but in our time carries a new urgency. The Psalms offer one wonderful way to know our God.

Our times burst with busyness. There are many enriching things on our "to-do list". I have found the Psalms a prayer-gift for our times. Because of my love for poetry, I experience the Psalms as an extra-special connection to God.

Poetry has the power to express thoughts concisely, to unveil beauty, and to create a world beyond experience with mere words. I feel that the Psalms image God in that way, and we know that images reflect the relationship. I hope to share that love and that connection with *you*.

Spirit Script invites you, a seeker, to discover without and within your relationship with the God of love, joy and co-creation.

Finally, here's an Amen, Alleluia to that invitation from Pedro Arupe, former superior general of the Jesuit community—I paraphrase his words:

Nothing is more exciting than falling in love with God! Who you are in love with seizes your imagination, affects everything. It will decide what will get you out of bed in the morning, what you will do with your evenings, how you spend your weekends, what you read, whom you know, what breaks your heart, and what amazes you with joy and gratitude.

Fall in Love. Why not?

Briefing: Getting to Know You God

No matter what our religious convictions, it is evident that we live, move, and have our being in a relationship with God.

Theologians rest their teaching on John 15:15, concluding that the word most appropriate for that relationship is *friendship*.

My experience says, "Yes!" to their teaching.

On a simpler, more imaginative level, you might sing two oldies: "You've Got a Friend" and "Getting to Know You."

Grace and these reflections will stimulate fresh insights.

God's Biography

Have you ever thought of the Psalms as chapters of God's biography?

We can thank our ancestors for faith for this treasure. Moreover, despite their human limitations, those who wrote the Psalms gave an account that is credible as the work of the Holy Spirit and confirmed as a mirror of our own life experiences.

One day, some years ago, you spoke your first word. Perhaps, it was "Daddy". (The joy your dad felt in this newly named role must have been unmatched.)

Years pass, your name is called, maybe even, "cum laude", as you receive your degree. There is a double joy: joy for you and for your Dad.

I remember that when I became "Sister", my parents rejoiced—that day and ever after.

Names open doors to identify and mark the intimacy of relationships. Marriage means, or at least it used to, the bride becoming Mrs. _____, and becoming entwined with the identity of her new husband.

But who can name our God, who is infinite and beyond imagining? The gospel of John ends by saying, "There are many things that Jesus did; yet, if they were written about in detail, I doubt there would be enough room in the entire world to hold the books to record them."

Names tend to change as experiences and relationships grow. As a child, I called God, "my Father." Having a warm and loving earthly Dad, that name came easily and naturally.

When I began teaching, I learned that love-deprived children didn't find it so simple to think of our heavenly Father as being near and loving.

Names being identifiers, growing in wisdom with grace, how we address God will most likely change. At one time, "Triune God" fit my image. This name was replaced, however, by "Beloved", "Beauty", "Engaging Mystery", and "Spirit".

One retreat director suggested that we begin with God's own naming—I AM—and continue with what was true for us.

Amazingly, Psalm 23 reminds us that the goodness and love of this great God follow us every day of our lives. In the rich detail of the Psalms, we learn that those whom no one cares for are precious in God's eyes, and He loves us *all* with a Love that is lavish and forever. The list goes on without end so that with St. John, we can proclaim,

> "Of his fullness, we have all had a share, love following upon love."

Have your names for God changed? What is that name now?

Reflection

There is a phrase from Psalm 23 that embodies these changes and begs our trust. It is "You are true to your name." Might it not be a help to know a bit more clearly the God "who first loved us?" The following questions are starters:

> Who wipes away all sin" Ps 103:3
> Who embraces all life? Ps 36:7
> Whose love encircles me? Ps 31:22

Pray the Psalms

> Your care lifts my spirit. Ps 94:19
> Restore to us the light of your presence. Ps 80:20
> God freed me from all my fears. Ps 34:5

Hunger for God

I have a habit of purchasing books simply because of their titles. Among my collection are: *Finding What You Didn't Lose*, *Seeing Beyond Z*, *The Sound of Blue*, and *Hailstones and Halibut Bones*. Sometimes, the content doesn't measure up to my expectations.

But not so for a recent one called *God Hunger* by John Kervan. If you're a searcher on the journey to God, this book will whet your appetite.

Mothers hear children complaining of hunger often, even if what they are asking for isn't really food. Growing up with five brothers, in their teens, I remember how the boys would get up from dinner asking, "Mom, is there anything to eat?"

Couldn't Lenten fasting be re-worded: "Hungry—For"? Furthermore, the very thing we promise to let go begins to consume our thoughts. How does that longing for sweets, liquor, or whatever, measure up with our God-longing? Is God a deep longing? Here's a little taste of what I mean by hungering for God. It's from C.S. Lewis: "This hunger (for God) is better than any other fullness; this poverty better than all other wealth."

Do the following lines from Psalm 63 speak to you?

> "O God, you are my God—
> for you I long.
> For you, my body yearns,
> for you my soul thirsts,
> Like a land parched, lifeless,
> and without water."

Perhaps, you're thinking, "But how? My day overflows with busyness involving my family, friends, work, and even a 'little' me." Though each of us has to iron out the details, a workable solution can be found in praying the psalms. Remember a line, a phrase, or just a word from a psalm that expresses your longing. Try praying it throughout the day and before you retire, thanking God for the remembering, regardless of whether the times were many or just a few.

It's amazing how, over time, your trying will deepen to yearning, and match what C. S. Lewis observed, "This hunger for God is better than any other fullness, this poverty better than all other wealth."

A final thought: Who can surpass God's love for YOU?

Reflection

The world spreads a sumptuous feast. How about nourishing our "God Hunger"?

Who or what feeds your longing for God? In what ways have you tasted God's goodness?

Remember: With God, there is always more.

Pray the Psalms

Drink in the richness of God. Ps 34:9

The Lord is my Shepherd; I need nothing more. Ps 23:1

Awakening

Remember the commercial, "The best part of waking up is Folgers in your cup?"

Is it? Is it really? Could it be more likely that indeed there is another "waking up"—awakening to a new day fresh with possibilities?

Thomas Merton, a poet and Trappist monk, describes the awakening of the birds in this way: "The first chirps of the waking birds mark the *le point vierge* (the virgin point) of the dawn…a moment of awe and inexpressible innocence, when the Father in perfect silence opens their eyes." They speak to Him, wondering if it is time to *be*. He tells them, "Yes." Then, they, one by one, wake and begin to sing.

Perhaps Merton's description is too richly poetic to image your awakening. Perhaps yours really is "for the birds." However, one thing is certain: God is there: ever present to us, too.

"Let morning announce your love." (Ps 143:8)

Morning is a sacred moment in our lives. Morning is a time to enter into wakefulness—awareness—that will keep us connected throughout the day to the God who came to bring us life to the full.

What if the day's busyness sweeps us away and we forget about God? We can rely on St. Paul's belief that "the Spirit helps us in our weakness... the Spirit intercedes with sighs too deep for words" (Romans 8:26).

Then, just before drifting off to sleep, we can consciously return and rest in the presence of our loving God. This kind of remembering will root us in a rhythm of awareness.

Perhaps, as you read this page, you thought,

- "Sounds wonderful!"
- "Wish I could!"
- "Maybe I should!"

When that happens, not just reading, but truly believing begins to emerge. What follows is a beginning, or a fleshing-out, of your wishes.

Lines from two Psalms come to mind: "The Lord never forgets the poor." Ps 9:19 and "God is here right beside me. I cannot be shaken." Ps. 16:8. Expanding our definition of "poor" to include "spiritual need or desire", we have in both Psalms a perfect reason for beginning the awareness practice.

Reflection

Once awake, ask the Spirit for an abiding sense of awareness.

Try asking yourself the following questions:

Who came to bring life to the full? Who promised to be with us always? Who loved first?

Pray the Psalms

God gives us life again. Ps 80:19
You never desert us Lord. Ps 94:14
Shine your love on us each day. Ps 90:14
All day, I sing your glory. Ps 71:8

Colors That Glorify

Year after year, fireworks at neighborhood parks spread their thrill. Brilliant blues, shocking reds, impetuous yellows splash across the night sky in awesome patterns while purples and greens also appear in breath-taking designs. There is a chorus of "Ooohs" and "Aahs" and then, sighs of regret at the last burst of wonder.

Think of a sunrise, a sunset—color glorified by light. Think of rows of lighted Christmas trees, a field of poppies, lakes of blue, or a pride of peacocks. Think of what wonders, what beauty, what life color brings to things.

In her delightful book of poems, *Hailstones and Halibut Bones,* Mary O'Neil writes:

> "Like acrobats on a high trapeze
> The Colors pose and bend their knees
> Twist and turn and leap and bend
> Into shapes and feelings without end.
> Colors dance and Colors sing
> And Colors laugh and Colors cry
> And they make you feel
> Every feeling there is."

Think of this world without color!

Caught up in the thrill of creativity, it would seem that God thinks in rainbows. By a word, a smile, a gesture, you, too, can help create a beautiful world. You can change a gray day into bright yellow possibilities.

Reflection

As your awareness grows, and you begin to notice in a new way those things long present, thank our creative God. If someone is feeling blue, add a splash of yellow—the sun's/Son's color. Find ways to color the day beautiful. Find ways to know different people. Psalms 31:25, 30:12 and 117:2 provide prayer power to make such things happen.

Pray the Psalms

Be strong, be brave all who wait for God. Ps 31:25

You changed my anguish into this joyful dance, pulled off my sackcloth gave me bright new robes. Ps 30:12

Strong the love embracing us. Faithful the Lord forever. Ps 117:2.

Evergreen Love

When the leaves change color, October's splendor is eye-catching. However, October isn't the only month to admire trees. Have you ever taken a long look at evergreens during winter? Think how the evergreen stands straight and steadfast through the weathers of all seasons. In this way, it proclaims that life and hope are forever.

How like the evergreen is our God! The American novelist John Updike reflects, "God is a bottomless encouragement to our faltering frightened being."

Who needs encouragement? I know I do. Those who try to be listeners do. Those who go to work each day do.

In fact, to get out of bed and begin the day leaves all of us open to regrets, decisions, concern tiredness, and a whole long list of negativity. But, there is also faith—the reassuring truth that says you are loved with an everlasting and unconditional love.

Scripture assures us that God's love is unending: "God's fidelity outlasts the heavens."

And God promises, "I honor my pledge of love, guard my covenant forever." Ps 89:29

"Forever" is a long, long time; in fact, it is beyond time.

Reflection

Considering your own experiences of God's faithful love, what do you find?

- Someone to lean into for strength?
- Someone there for all seasons?
- Someone to offer protection from life's storms?
- Someone who loved you so much that he died on a tree to give us life forever?

Finish the list with the remembrance of your personal experiences. Keep *evergreen* in your line of vision.

Pray the Psalms

God's ways are faithful love. Ps 25:10
I am sure God is here right beside me. Ps 16:8
Your sure and tender care protects me always. Ps 40:12

Extravagant Love

When I was hospitalized and quite ill, pain, pills, and yucky experiences peppered my days. I thought of the homebound and their caregivers. Their grit, their courage, and, of course, their faith, were a source of encouragement for me.

And, wonder of wonders, I realized that, despite hard times, goodness—full and plenty—enfolds us. The God of Life fills our days with extravagant love. It is awareness of such goodness that I would like to awaken in you.

For starters, consider the gift of the morning with all its possibilities to love and be loved. You wake in a world teeming with life, to a world wrapped in beauty. Then, there are the people in your life who, in myriad ways, give you a reason to hope. Look for life, and know that you'll find possibilities in each day.

It seems to me that among the many gifts with which our extravagant God has blessed us, wonder shines most brightly.

> Abraham Heschel believed, "Awareness of the divine begins with wonder."
>
> Perhaps, The Carpenters wouldn't mind if I borrowed some lines from *Top of the World*."

"Such a feelin' comin' over me; there is wonder in most everything I see…

In the leaves on the trees and the touch of the breeze, there's a pleasin' sense of happiness for me.

I'm on the top of the world lookin' down on creation

Your Love's put me at the top of the world."

God, the Source of Life, is always in our midst breathing energy into our hearts, Take the time to find the wonder in everything you see—and feel "on top of the world".

Reflection

Think of ways to:

- Take note of smiles, words and small pleasures.
- Look for (and know that you'll find) possibilities in the day.
- Try to do some deep breathing while remembering God, who breathed life into you.
- Try to be aware of the sounds of life.

Pray the Psalms

Wrap me again in mercy. Ps 71:21
Now is the moment. Ps 65:2
Listen today to God's voice. Ps 95:8

Real Prayer

"For all that has been—Thanks! To all that shall be—Yes!"

You recognize, don't you, Dag Hammarskjold's prayer? What a way to greet each day—unless, perhaps, you have a prayer of your own—a real prayer.

"Real" prayer keeps us connected to the lives we lead, coming from communion with the God who promised to be with us always and in all ways. "Real" prayer lets God break into our day from within us. "Real" prayer makes us aware that there is no *ordinary*—all is *extraordinary*.

Quiet opens us to such reflection and resolution. These days I hear others saying that they are tied to their calendars: waking up, they check to see what has to be done.

I confess to being sort of like them; however, my first stop is my prayer rocker to be centered in Triune God, the Holy One. Knowing that all around me and within me, life emerges embraced in God's loving presence. The day will unfold with joy, challenge, and maybe even sorrow.

Just know that prayer is a good place to begin.

Reflection

How "real" is <u>your</u> prayer? Where does your God of prayer live? In your heart? In your head? In your day? Why not:

- Pray a Psalm of longing, a real prayer of longing. Ps 63
- Pray a Psalm of trust as your real prayer of trust. Ps 103
- Pray a Psalm of joy. Ps 98.
- Match your joy with that expressed in Psalm 98.

Pray the Psalms

Psalm 92: 2, 3 expresses well the circle of prayer that each day offers:

> "How good to thank you, Lord."
> "How good to sing your love at dawn."
> "How good to sing your faithfulness at dusk."

God Is

Old Turtle by Douglas Wood is one of my favorite children's books. Both the story and the illustrations are works of beauty. The story tells of a people who could not remember who they were or where God was. Throughout the story, Old Turtle reminds creatures of their Maker with words that cause the reader's heart to melt and glow. The illustrations are bold and engaging.

To the fish in the sea, Old Turtle said, "God is indeed deep" and to the mountains, "much higher than high." Old Turtle tells the ant and the star, "God is gentle and powerful, above all things and within all things."

John O' Donohue, Irish teacher and poet, suggests this dearest thought, "There is a quiet light that shines in every heart. It is what illuminates our minds to see beauty, to seek possibility and our hearts to love life."

I name that light "the blessing of God's presence".

O'Donohue goes on to assure us that *blessing* breathes spirit which suffering cannot quench, which is ours each day for always.

This is how Old Turtle concludes, "God is all that we dream of and all that we seek. All that we come from and all that we can find, 'GOD IS.'" Wow! Think of that!

Reflection

Everything is God-blessing, and so God is also everywhere. While you're reading this and remembering God and the many blessings that overwhelm you, nourish you, and delight you, why not consider how to be more aware and grateful?

Pray the Psalms

My whole life, give praise. Ps 146:2
All that is alive praise. Praise the Lord. Ps 150:6
I ponder all your wonderful works. Ps 145:5

Open House

"Open House" is a tempting sign for me, though it goes without saying that I never have and never will buy a house.

I go in just to discover what's inside. I have a feeling that I am not alone in this fascination. What about you?

And how about this? Our God has been inviting us in many ways and over eternity to come to His "open house."

In both the Old and New Testaments, God opens wide the doors emblazoned:

"Come to Me."

What kinds of treasures might we discover if we walked through the ever-open doors of God's home/heart?

My copy of *Show Yourself to My Soul* by Rabindranath Tagore, is worn, patched, and well-underlined.

With perhaps the exception of his contemporary, Gandhi, Tagore is identified as the most famous Indian. Better yet, beginning deep within, recognizing his own limitations and vulnerability, Tagore engaged in the birth of his cosmic vision for humanity. His prayer-poems remain relevant for any spiritual seeker.

As you know, Jesus invited us to *come* when we're weary, to *come* and see. The following lines are a taste of Tagore's *come* ~

"Come, show yourself
to my soul
in ever new ways…"

Tempting isn't it? Then, what if we let those God-images shape our responses to each day.

Reflection

Why not let this truth, the truth of these images, lure you like an "Open House" sign on green, green grass?

Pray the Psalms

Because our God lifts us, the fallen, I will reach out and _____.
Trust God and do good. Ps 37:3
Because our God loves forever, I will wrap each day in love by _____.
You bless the just, O God. Ps 5:13
Because God keeps promises, I will _____.
God, our God, has blessed us. Ps 67:7

Unconditional Love

"How do I love thee? Let me count the ways."

You probably recognize these lines from Elizabeth Barrett Browning's *Sonnet 43*. They are lines almost ancient but with applications that can make them refreshingly new. How about using Browning's quotation with a different twist? Imagine God as the speaker. Hear God saying to you, "How do I love thee?" and you responding, "Let me count the ways."

We know, of course, that God's love is unconditional, and the ways of God's loving are countless—beyond our wildest imaginings. St. Paul, writing to the Ephesians, says it like this,

"His power now at work in us can do immeasurably more than we ask or imagine."

It would seem that attempting to become more aware of God's loving ways would surely increase our gratitude—and a grateful heart is a happy heart.

These three questions taken from the Psalms will hopefully tickle your memory and prompt an appropriate response. Who fills the earth with love (Ps 33:5)? Who never lets me down (Ps 33:4)? Who shows me wonderful love (Ps 17:7)?

"Sounds good," you say, "but what about the difficult days, the less cheery days—the teary days?" No question, it's tough to trust during the hard times of loss. Yet, God asks our trust because He is Emmanuel—a permanent presence—with us always and in <u>ALL</u> ways.

Reflection

It goes without saying: Our God is an extravagant Giver whose ways of loving are infinite.

Pray the Psalms

> God stays near broken hearts. Ps 34:19
> God shows me wonderful love. Ps 17:7
> God frees me from all my fears. Ps 34:5

Closer in Love

"Perhaps Love," John Denver's song, is one that I could hear Jesus humming. It goes like this, do you remember?

> "Love is like an open door
> invites you to come closer
> wants to show you more."

Don't these lines describe Jesus, who said of himself, "I am the way" (John 14:6)? And doesn't his invitation, "Come and see" (John 1:39) continue to invite us today?

What I'm suggesting is spending some quality time focused on God as Love.

"Love…invites you to come closer." What will that amazing invitation mean for you? Listening/Reconciliation? Cheerful responses? Accepting reversals?

- Come closer in love: Be forgiving.
- Come closer in love: Respond cheerfully.
- Come closer in love: Be a peacemaker.

Reflection

"Love wants to show you more," says the rest of the line in the song.

You live in exciting times; especially if you are a seeker, and you must be if you're reading this.

Author open us to a whole new understanding of Creator God, others, *YOU* and our universe.

These understandings offer a worldview that will change your relationships, your prayer. "What if? Why not?"

What do you suppose Jesus wants to show you?

"Eye has not seen. Ear has not heard," writes St. Paul.

You just cannot imagine. But why not try?

Pray the Psalms

O God, welcome us with love. Ps 79:8
Favor and bless us, Lord. Ps 67:2

Briefing: God Moments

"You understand so little of what is around you because you use so little of what is within you," said St. Hildegard of Bingen. Her insight, which is so wise and so practical, gives us a wonderful way to be aware of the graced moments of each day. "Turn to the Spirit, who dwells within," she suggests, "the Spirit waiting to energize us in unbelievable ways."

The following reflections are meant to open the door to some possibilities of awareness and the reality of God's presence and promise.

Burst of Radiance

Attending an October retreat, I expect God to be evident in a riot of fall color. I count as one of the many blessings of this retreat the joy of walking in acres of vibrant beauty.

Some time ago, while going to a retreat in Canada, some of the retreat-goers and I happened upon a wondrous nature scene. We saw dozens of spider webs among a cluster of evergreens literally.

The webs were perfectly formed—not a thread broken. The sun gave the webs the appearance of spun glass. Droplets of dew clung to the webs like tiny diamonds.

The sight was awesome. Most of us dashed back to the retreat house for our cameras.

However, by the time we returned, the webs had evaporated along with the breathless wonder of the scene. That can also happen in a "God moment."

Fleeting, spontaneous, graced-gift, possible, real, elusive, and indescribable are some of the adjectives that fit *God moments*. Yet, as St. Augustine once said, "God is closer to your soul than you are yourself."

Perhaps you have been gifted with God moments and can identify with those adjectives, or maybe your experience responds, "Nothing happens."

My experience says, "God is an *extravagant Giver*."

The sixteenth-century mystic, John of the Cross, says, "Silence is God's first language." Practice silence to make space in your life for God's gifts.

Reflection

The question is: How shall we greet that burst of radiance—our God?

Why not trust God and expect his giving?

Pray the Psalms

Most high God, you are awesome. Ps 47:3
Changed my sadness to joy. Ps 30:12
God—my glory, my safety. Ps 62:8

The Lord's Look

"God looked at *everything* he made and God found it *very* good."

That oft-repeated line from the Genesis creation story tells a lot about God's look. The writer Mark Van Doren reflects that, when God looks at a soul, God *makes it beautiful*. The look of God! The look of God! The look that is focused on making us all that we can be.

Recall the gospels that show the power of Jesus' look when he invites, challenges, heals, forgives, and loves tenderly.

"When Jesus came to the spot, he looked up and said, 'Zacchaeus hurry down. I mean to stay at your house today.'" (Luke 19:5)

"Then Jesus looked at him with love…" (Mark 10:21)

"He has looked upon his servant…all ages shall call me blessed." (Luke 1:48)

"He looked up to heaven… and said, 'Be opened.'" (Mark 7:34)

"The Lord turned and looked at Peter…" (Luke 22:61)

"The Lord was moved with pity upon seeing her and said to her,

'Do not cry.'" (Luke 7:13)

As you reflect on these gospel stories, be sure to add one more:

God looks at you not just once, though it's extravagant, but again and again.

Why not really believe and embrace that God whose *look* invites you to grow, to open your heart to a new creation?

Reflection

The same Jesus desires that we reach out to others in their need. If we but ask and believe, we, too, have power in our look.

What difference would it make to try to see those around us as Jesus sees them? How about looking at yourself each day as God looks at you?

Pray the Psalms

> I walk with you God in the light of your life. Ps 56:14
> Inspire me to learn your wisdom, O God. Ps 119:73

TRUST

When summer has surrendered to autumn, leaves have relinquished their greenness to become gloriously red, orange, and gold. Their letting go has given us a new and wondrous nature scene.

There's a true incident about a young girl during a solo flight who lost control: her Cessna 150 began a wild spin towards the earth. Despite her panic, the young pilot remembered her instructor's words, "If you ever go into a spin in a Cessna 150, just let go of the controls. It's built to fly on its own."

She did let go—and survived.

When my subconscious thoughts try to assert themselves, "I'm going to accomplish everything on my list—TODAY!" it doesn't take much imagination to know how I greet interruptions.

Providentially, while reading *The Unbearable Wholeness of Being* by Ilia Delio, the following lines struck me, "The life of Jesus shows us that to live with the confines of the expected, which seems to provide stability, security, and certainty, is to be dead even while alive; to be exposed to the unexpected is to be open to the creativity of life...."

Scripture encourages us seventy times to "fear not," and gives us fifty times the reason why: "God can be trusted."

Reflections

Why not try to wake up with this thought? "In you, O Lord, I put my trust." (Ps 31:15)

Then, try to surrender to whatever the day holds. Letting go that way means leaning on God's power. Expect a day beyond your imagination. Let fall leaves be a reminder of what can happen to you when and if....

Pray the Psalms

You soothe my head with oil; my cup is more than full. Ps 23:5

You encircle me with songs of freedom. Ps 32:7

You, God, healed me. Ps 30:3

Light of the World

In John 8, we hear Jesus sayng, "I am the Light of the world." What did Jesus mean?

"I Am" is the special Hebrew name for God. The Hebrew translates: "He who is always there." When Jesus says, "I am the Light of the world," he is making a promise, "I will be with you always."

One way that Jesus has promised to be with us is as "light." Jesus' light will help us see people and things as he sees them. Wow, what a difference! That same light draws goodness from within us. We enter into good, happy relationships. We reflect God's light to one another, and there's a warm difference at home and beyond.

Remember a spectacular fireworks display? Experience tells us that God's responses are more brilliant and varied than the most fabulous fireworks.

Can you predict with certainty what God will do? Hasn't God at times responded with some unexpected designs? And hasn't God's love sometimes surprised you in breathtaking sparklers of delight?

There we have it—a new image of the God of Light as colorful, as spontaneous, and as awesome as fireworks. Psalm 27 will tell you all about it.

Reflection

Coming to this new image of the Holy, how can you become more wholly YOU?

Pray the Psalms

Where/with whom do I find light? Give light to my eyes that I may not sleep in death. Ps 13:4
How can I increase my awareness of Jesus' light? Send your light and truth. Ps 43:3
To whom will I bring light/Light? The revelation of your words shed light. Ps 119:130

Eternal in Time

Daylight Savings Time originated as a way to save fuel and, consequently, money. Those living on the lighter side of life welcome the longer day as an opportunity to enjoy nature and more recreation.

There is an Irish proverb that says, "God created time and plenty of it." Why is it, then, that most of us have too much to do and too little time in which to do it? The familiar expressions of how we use time provoke curiosity. We say that we are: "spending time", "making time", "taking time" "wasting time", and (horrors!) "killing time". Incarnation means encountering God in time. It follows then, that what is truly important about time is its God-content, and how we use time becomes an important issue. To quote Abraham Heschel, "Spiritual life begins to decay when we fail to sense the grandeur of what is eternal in time."

"…The grandeur of what is eternal in time"—finding God in the here and now.

There are different ways to get in touch with that aspect of time. Why not focus on one way of doing that—by *spending time with God*? This way involves the practice of spending even a moment—a sacred moment—to be present to God. It means making time for sacred moments throughout the day. With each sacred moment, use human time to open up space for God in your day.

Reflection

In Matthew's gospel, we learn that Jesus made time for such moments. Jesus withdrew to be with God the Father. The Greek word for "withdraw" has shades of meaning, one of which is withdrawing in order to make room for the persons and situations encountered upon return. "*Now* is a gift of God; perhaps, that is why it is called *the present*."

Pray the Psalms

> My whole being is at rest. Ps 131:2
> Fill us at daybreak with your love. Ps 90:14

Wondrous Differences

"It has been said that we could learn a lot from a box of crayons: some are sharp, some are pretty, some are dull, some have weird names and all are different colors… but they all have to learn to live in the same box."

Isn't that quote by Robert Fulghum the best of wisdom in a down- to-earth metaphor?

Of course, the obvious conclusion is that we wouldn't want them to be the same color. Their variety is their appeal.

All of creation convinces us that our creator God is an artist with a workbox filled to overflowing. Look at the flowers closest to you. Then, picture meadows, arboretums, florists, and grocery stores—all beautiful with different kinds of flowers. All nature displays variety.

Singing the traditional hymn "O Lord my God, when I in awesome wonder, consider all the worlds Thy hands have made," we begin to realize how vast, yet, how wondrous, is God's world of differences.

Think of different people that you meet within a day. For that matter, consider how you differ from your brother or sister. We do, indeed, live in a world of many cultures, religions, values, and views.

Isn't it amazing how five people can present five different points of view? Moving closer to the nitty-gritty of every day, are you ever asked to give up your perfect solution in favor of another? Different people and different situations provide us with what we might consider our box of crayons.

Reflection

With all our differences—cultures, religions, values, views—it would seem that our challenge is "to learn to live in the same box"—this strikingly beautiful, wonderful world. Why not notice and praise God in the extraordinary variety of creation that surrounds you? "Drink in the richness of God." Ps 34:9

Pray the Psalms

Notice and praise God in the extraordinary variety of creation. I ponder all your wonderful works. Ps 145:5

Welcome someone or some situation that you find "different." Listen to God today. Ps 95:8

Try doing an ordinary task in a different way. Lord, you see to the heart of things. Ps 49:4

Jesus, Our Friend

"When he saw the crowds, he went up on the mountainside. After he sat down, his disciples gathered around him...."

These lines from Matthew's gospel are so warm and inviting. Picture the scene. Jesus sitting down with his friends, his disciples gathered around him. Can you see yourself as one of the circle? As friends would, they are sharing:

- the hard and silly things that happened that day;
- future hopes and dreams—those seeds that nourish us when the daily routine wears us down;
- secrets? Yes. With real friends, we eventually come around to sharing the secrets of our souls.

And when it comes time to part, friends have special ways of expressing just what a gift it is to have someone who really cares, who really listens.

The Psalms are meant to help us sit with Jesus, our friend. Remember the Psalms are just suggestions. Did you ever try to shape them to mirror your relationship?

From the reflection, take the first question. Here is an example of how simple, yet meaningful, the change can be. You know Psalm 23 by heart, don't you? By changing the image of "shepherd" to "friend", this Psalm becomes a *personal* prayer. "Lord God, you are my Friend.

I want for nothing.

You fill my day with goodness, giving me energy to begin again.

You revive my spirit."

Reflection

Someone once asked: "How does an apple ripen?" How? It just sits in the sun/Son!

"I am sure God is here, right beside me," says Psalm 16:8. Talk with your Friend AND listen, too.

Pray the Psalms

Wrap me again in mercy. Ps 71:21

You give my heart more joy than all the grain and wine. Ps 4:8

Exploding Love

Fireworks are amazing and paradoxical—breathtakingly beautiful, thoroughly enjoyable, yet powerfully dangerous.

I know someone who has been described as a "firecracker". She can be charming and amusing, but also explosive with no warning—a "short fuse". It's an apt description—just incomplete.

Perhaps it's true to say that we all have the potential for a similar description, yet is any one of us all gentle, all kindness, all *anything*? There is, I believe, more to who we are than we know; and yet, to become a whole/holy person is what we're all about.

At times that can seem like an oversized order unless we understand, as did Thomas Merton, monk and life-writer, that "being oneself is all that is required for sanctity wholeness/holiness, all that God expects. All else can be done equally well or better by others."

John Shea, spiritual author and speaker, reflecting on the topic, takes us further. He writes, "At one time or another, we feel great love in the center of ourselves, in the soul space as it opens and receives the love of the Spirit. This love explodes and pushes us into the outer world."

In the phrase "explodes and pushes us into the outer world," do you recognize the pattern of *Spirit Script?* We go within (the Reflection and Psalms) in order to discover a way of being without.

Reflection

Remembering the Spirit's presence within, there is no giving up, only giving in. Just imagine what amazing things can happen when you are open to the Eternal Flame within you.

Pray the Psalms

Shine your love on us each dawn. Ps 90:14
God will cover you like a nesting bird. Ps 91:4
The Lord delights in saving a helpless people. Ps 149:4

CHRIST IS THERE

Most of us know that it's fairly easy to feel good and to feel the goodness of God when all goes well. Times of pain and aloneness are a different matter. We struggle to find God in the mystery of pain.

It seems to me that the challenge is to believe in the Divine Indwelling, Emmanuel, God-with-us, and to try to grow in that awareness where we are, how we are NOW. God's love is all around us even when we don't feel it or understand it. Remember how beautifully the poet Gerard Manley Hopkins expressed it? "Christ plays in 10,000 places, lovely in limbs and lovely in eyes, not his."

So when you try, Christ is there. When you reach out, Christ is there. When you're challenged, Christ is there. When you're forgiving, Christ is there. When you turn a "no-win" into a blessing, Christ is there.

Psalm 95 includes the following line: "This is our God, our shepherd, we are the flock led with care." That image of God as a shepherd is not startling since Psalm 23 makes it familiar and time-honored.

Reflection

Keeping in mind Hopkins' belief in the infinite presence of God, what new images and experiences might be ours if we would take only the first part of the Psalm line, "This is our God..." and be open to letting our day complete the sentence. Why not give it a try?

Pray the Psalms

God works wonders. Rejoice! Be glad! Ps 126:3
Your goodness is boundless. Ps 71:19
You show me the road to life; boundless joy at your side forever. Ps 16:11

Beautiful Questions

The poet e.e. cummings wrote, "Always the beautiful answer. Who asks a beautiful question?"

Questions are remarkable stimulators. We find Jesus doing this in the gospels. His questions are beautiful in the way that they open minds and spirits to hidden potential, to a broader vision and to spiritual quests. Jesus' questions have a way of provoking, engaging, compelling, and always challenging his listeners.

Interestingly enough, our own times leave seekers questioning.

Scripture imaged God as ever-abiding; the new cosmology presents God as ever-emerging. Has your image of God changed?

Exploring new understandings of God means changing. What feelings do these changes evoke?

How has this exploring deepened your relationships with the world, others, and even yourself?

The following words of T.S. Eliot seem apropos:

> "Were I to sit—to listen—to be
> Would I allow the Lord
> To *question* me
> To be present to me?"

Reflection

This is a beautiful invitation, and the question I would propose is what Jesus asked of the blind Bartimaeus, "What do you want me to do for you?" (Mark 11:31)

Pray the Psalms

Show me a sign of your love. Ps 86:17
I answer those who call me. Ps 91:15
My people, listen. Ps 81:14

Hidden in Plain Sight

Have you ever really thought about the expression "hidden in plain sight?" For sure, nature has wonders that are "hidden in plain sight."

Spring with new growth—tiny green leaves popping through dark, hard branches or daffodils trumpeting the season—calls for particular perception instead of take-it-for-granted looking.

If you were to try to really look at the wonders in nature that surround you and to remember the Creator of them all, Psalm 19 could be kind of a mood setter.

> "The sky tells us the glory of God,
> tells the genius of God's work.
> Day carries the news to day,
> night brings the message to night,
> without a word, without a sound,
> without a voice being heard,
> yet, their message fills the world…
> their news reaches its rim."

The Psalm goes on to describe the sun as a bridegroom or "athlete eager to run the race." Have you ever really thought about the miracle of the sun? And what about the miracles of the Son? Perhaps, a lack of awareness or a lack of familiarity with God's ways keeps us missing the many revelations of Emmanuel, God-with-us.

Reflection

Ask God to open the eyes of your heart. What would help you to be more aware of the creativity, the beauty, and the glory of God that surrounds you on your daily path? What is blocking your heart-vision?

Pray the Psalms

A new world of wonders! God is with us! Ps 126:3
The trees of the forest sing at God's coming. Ps 96:13
Lord, I marvel at what you do. Ps 92:6

What is Blessing?

Scripture defines blessings as a communication from God. Simply put, when we bless someone, we ask that God enter that person in a very special way.

John O'Donohue, the Irish teacher and poet, captures the essence of blessing with diaphanous intimacy. "Blessing," O'Donohue writes, "is a gracious invocation where the human heart pleads with the divine heart."

Blessing someone calls forth that person's innate goodness. We do that by using a blessing gesture (placing hands on the person's head or shoulders) and praying that God bless the person.

Perhaps your family prayed grace before and after meals; perhaps, your family prayed a more festive grace at Thanksgiving, Christmas, Easter and other holidays.

"May God bless you" is the basic wording for personal blessings; however, sometimes you might want to be more specific or more elaborate. The following are some samples:

- "May the God of Peace be with you, stilling all your unrest."
- "May the God of Love be with you, filling your heart for giving."

- "May the God of Strength be with you, giving you courage to stand tall."
- "May the God of Mercy welcome you with open arms."
- "May our Creative God fill your heart with joyful song."

There are worlds of possibilities in this gift of blessing. Wouldn't it be a lovely way to gift the birthday person at the family party? It could even become a tradition.

Reflection

Your reflection on blessings will surely prompt ways to initiate this prayer in your family.

Pray the Psalms

> You welcome us with godly blessings. Ps 21:4
> I pour out my riches. Creation springs to life. Ps 85:13
> All my being bless the Lord. Ps 103:1

Images of God

I have a crystal suncatcher in my office window. It sends rainbows—strong, vibrant rainbows—dancing all around the office, even spilling out into the hall. On blustery cold days, it becomes a heart-warming presence. God's love is like that.

God's love is a dynamic, abiding presence; yet, a presence that our noisy, action-crammed world can muffle. That's why icons, holy pictures, and medals can be helpful in reminding us that we are never alone. Jesus promised to be with us always. (Matthew 28:20)

Possible reminders of the Holy presence are limitless. One of St. Hildegard of Bingen's images of God was "green dew." Green dew is typical of the imaginative person that Hildegard was.

What about you? What is it that reminds you of God?

Usually, it's best to choose something that is inconspicuous to others, something that you can keep close, maybe something that is already present. With mindful focus, it can become your reminder of Spirit.

Reflection

Finding <u>your</u> image of God, turn to it often during the day. In sunshine times, believing in God's nearness comes easy. In tough times, however, our faith becomes the crystal through which the sun/Son shines.

Pray the Psalms

> Show me a sign of your love. Ps 86:17
> Let your loveliness shine on us. Ps 90:17
> Comfort me with your love. Ps 119:76

Enticing Invitations

Is there anything more exhilarating than a fresh insight? I had just such an experience, and it revolved around this line, "The sayings of Jesus are NOT information but invitations."

What a soul-stirring awakening! I was peppered with joy and excitement for days. Before sharing this insight, I decided to check "invitation" in the dictionary. There were four definitions. How about this one? "Invite: to entice."

Wouldn't it be worthwhile to pursue that meaning of invite with your favorite saying of Jesus? Such an attempt would seem to me, not an effort, but rather, a gift that would deepen your relationship with Jesus.

Here is a sample of how you might do this. In Matthew 18:5, Jesus says, "Whoever welcomes a little child in my name, welcomes me." Do you hear the invitation in that remark? Can you hear the suggestion, the hope?

Reflection

The biblical word "anawim" is a timeless synonym for one made dependent. While on earth, Jesus made these "little people" the target of his love. Choosing this word, you will be amazed in how many ways and with how many people you might welcome Jesus in one day. Remember though, this is just a sample. Use your own favorite saying and RSVP to His invitation.

Pray the Psalms

God is here right beside me, I cannot be shaken. Ps 16:8

The Lord never forgets the poor. The Lord never lets their hope die. Ps 9:19

As your teacher, I watch out for you. Ps 32:8

Heart Work

Briefing: Heart Work

Scripture images the heart as the source of good and evil. In Luke's gospel, we read,

"A good person out of the store of goodness in his heart produces good, but an evil person out of the store of evil produces evil, for from the fullness of the heart, the mouth speaks."

Then, there's us, the in-betweens. Where is our help? It, too, is in our heart where we meet our God, who promised to be with us, and who said, "I will give you a new heart and place a new spirit within you, taking from your bodies your stony hearts and giving you a natural heart."

The ideas suggested in the following reflections are meant to help you follow the guidance of the Spirit.

Remember the song, "This time, change our hearts" by Rory Cooney? Sing it! Pray it! Believe it!

Noticing

You surely have heard the gospel story of the widow's mite many times. I have, too. Recently, however, one phrase of it really unfolded for me. The phrase is, "He happened to notice…." The "He" of course, is Jesus, and the "who" is a poor inconspicuous woman.

Considering the probable crowd of pilgrims in the temple, Jesus' perception was remarkable; but then, scripture notes that Jesus observed a variety of things: birds, fig trees, sky, hunger, hospitality—and the lack of it.

Nature opens the eyes of the blind with an expanse of color, sizes, and shapes. Nature coaxes us to take notice, to pay some attention to our "blind spots." (We all have them.) "The Lord pours out riches, our land springs to life" (Ps 85:13). Nature in its rich variety is a good starting place, but only a start.

How about noticing:

- the quiet person overlooked in conversation;
- the self-giving one often taken for granted;
- those who try but aren't often successful.

The following quote from the poet Rilke invites us to real growth. The parentheses are mine.

"The work of sight is done." (That's noticing.)
"Now do the heart work…." (That's responding.)

Reflection

How does Jesus see the individuals I take for granted? My family? Co-workers? Those who serve me—police, firemen, military, farmers, grocers (you name them)? What about those I exclude? Those I try to avoid?

Pray the Psalms

Teach me your ways, O Lord. Ps 119:135
God says, "I have wisdom you need to hear." Ps 49:4
I see to the heart of things. Ps 49:4

HEARTS

Hearts are the symbol of February. The card, candy, and floral industries have a way of touching even the hardest of hearts. Lent often occurs in February. In the early days, Lent was experienced as a solemn time, but as the focus moved from sin to the love that God has shown, I began to put more heart into it. How about you?

However, in the matter of hearts, Solomon, Israel's wise king, is not to be surpassed. You remember the story of how God appeared to Solomon in a dream.

God said to Solomon, "Ask something of me, and I will give it to you." Presented with this opportunity, what would you ask? Solomon asked for "an understanding heart." God replied, "Because you have asked for this—not for a long life for yourself, not for riches, not for the life of your enemies… I give you a heart so wise and understanding that there has never been anyone like you up to now and after you, there will be no one to equal you."

What kind of heart might you ask of God?

- Compassionate
- Faith-filled
- All-embracing
- Brave
- Happy?

Psalm 51 begs, "Creator, reshape my heart," and Jesus invites us, "Ask and you shall receive." So, why not ask?

Reflection

Read the story in 1 Kings 3. You'll discover that God gave Solomon an understanding heart and much more.

Pray the Psalms

Walk in God's ways. Ps 81:14
You are a God full of loyalty and love. Ps 86:15
The Lord pours out riches, our land springs to life. Ps 85:13

Breaking

As you know, the verb "break" has multiple definitions. Some positive and beautiful meanings are: "bring to light, discover, unfold, and open up."

Not long ago, a friend sent me this prayer:

> "Be with us, Lord, in the Breaking,
> In the Breaking of the Day,
> In the Breaking of the Bread,
> In the Breaking of our Lives."

Any beginning invites us into the unknown. However, even though we don't know exactly what the beginning will bring, it is certain that leaning into God's presence will make a difference. "God will cover you like a nesting bird" (Ps 91:4).

There's another possibility worth considering: What difference would it make if we found ways to be with others in their *breaking*? For example, what if we listened patiently? Really listened? Listened and offered to help? Remained faithful in tough times?

Perhaps, then, our prayer would go something like this:

"Be with me, Lord, in the unfolding of my true self,
In the breaking into new patterns of life.
Be with me, Lord.
For you alone can make me whole."

Reflection

Who needs encouragement that I could give?
Why not start today?

Pray the Psalms

God hears my cry. Ps 55:19
My lips speak your goodness. Ps 71:15

Giving Trees

There is a classic story called *The Giving Tree* by Shel Silverstein. Perhaps you have read it. The story tells how a tree gives itself unselfishly to a boy during his lifetime.

The Giving Tree is truly a story of unconditional love. The original giving tree is the cross.

As St. John writes, God's love was revealed in this way. He sent his only Son into the world that we might have new life—his life forever and ever. Though the cross is a Lenten focus, any time is a good time to share your gifts.

In John's gospel (14:12), Jesus shares a heart-expanding insight about giving.

"The one who believes in me will also do the works I do, and, in fact, will do *greater* works than these."

What were Jesus' works? Bringing comfort; encouragement; sharing meals—even providing them; loving; reaching out to children and those excluded, and speaking positively.

There are many more but, as St. John noted, there aren't enough books in the world to record them.

Shape your own "giving tree." With that kind of sharing, you could help others come closer to understanding what an extravagant giver God is.

Reflection

Let your gratitude for God's unconditional love color your way of giving to someone—time, attention, love, or even more concrete gifts, like food and donations.

Pray the Psalms

Praise the God of goodness, the God of lasting love. Ps 106:1

The poor will hear me and be glad. Ps 4:3

Look always for the power, the presence of God. Ps 105:4

Look down from heaven on this vine you placed. Ps 80:15

What are You Hoping For?

Despite their history of unfaithfulness, the Israelites remained anchored in hope. Granted that Israel's hope was centered on material prosperity for a long time. However, God gradually led his people to true hope. Israel's hope grew until it centered on God and culminated in Jesus, God's Word-made-flesh.

Theirs (and ours) is a story of kept promises—hope fulfilled—because even as God promises, God gives. With the fulfillment of Old Testament promises, new promises began to unfold—promises that far surpassed the old.

Can we hope for too much from God? St. Paul didn't think so. In fact, he believed "God can do immeasurably more than we can ask or imagine." The Psalms remind us of the kinds of gifts prompted by God's unconditional love and urge us to look always for the power, for the presence of God. (Ps 105:4)

Recently, I uncovered some new definitions for *grace*. One, in view of God's unconditional love, is this:

"Grace: doing the divine thing."

Deserving and grace are non-related. It goes without saying that to give unconditionally reflects God's kind of love.

Reflection

I offer a challenge—a challenge inspired by God, who gave us his greatest gift, Jesus while we were still sinners. The challenge is this: Try giving with no strings attached—no expectations of return—give unconditionally. This is the *Christ* spirit!

Pray the Psalms

God's love is forever. Ps 118:4
The Lord has remembered us and will bless us. Ps 115:12
You never desert your people, Lord. Ps 94:14

Awesome Words

Some words are too awesome for comprehension. Have you ever experienced such a phenomenon? The word "mercy" is like that for me. Even the dictionary definition carries a certain incredulity: "compassion that forbears punishing even when justice demands it, or that extends help even to the lowliest or most undeserving."

How then, may we comprehend *mercy* as the *living* word—tender compassion of our God? We find answers in scripture and literature confirming that God's mercy is without limits and everlasting.

"The Lord God bestows mercy down to the thousand generation on those who love him." (Exodus 20:6)

"You who fear the Lord, hope for good things, for lasting joy and mercy. Study the generations long past and understand:

> Has anyone hoped in the Lord and been disappointed?
>
> Has anyone preserved in trust and been forsaken?" (Sirach 2:7-10)

Shakespeare described mercy as "a gentle rain". He found it to be a double blessing for us. Mercy blesses both the giver and the receiver.

Reflection

Actually, the tender mercy of our God is beyond our wildest imaginings. Yet, at some time, haven't all of us experienced it?

How has God's mercy been present to you?

How will you make that mercy present to others?

As the Psalmist proclaims: "Praise this awesome God whose mercy lasts a lifetime." Ps 30:6

Pray the Psalms

My God, you are my light, a lamp for my darkness. Ps 18:29

The Lord speaks out, "I will act now for the poor are broken." Ps 12:6

All you touch comes alive. Ps 65:12

Flowers in Bloom

Have you ever noticed how more often than not *quiet* is the adjective used to describe a garden? Perhaps, the garden is a place of quiet for you. Yet, true gardeners are also aware of bustling activity there, especially during pollination. The bees and the butterflies are surely engaged in a sort of important whispering busyness as they deposit the pollen, which causes even more flowers to bloom.

The other day, I happened upon one of my favorite quotations from St. John of the Cross, "Where there is no love, put love, and you will find love." St. John's idea reminded me of how the flowers need the help of the bees and butterflies in order to come to full bloom. Similarly, aren't there people within the circle of our day who need a "word of pollination"—a reminder just how loved they are and how loving we are all called to be?

The new universe story reminds us that in our connectedness, we are co-creators participating in the divine unfolding of life.

Reflection

How would you feel making St. John's words come alive, "bringing love where there is seemingly no love?" By unselfishly giving love, you will experience a deep-down joy though not necessarily from the one receiving your love. There is this guarantee: If you open your heart, God's love will bloom there.

Pray the Psalms

> Bless God who forgives your sin. Ps 103:3
> I sing to you. O Lord, sing your love. Ps 101:1

PATIENCE

Impatiens! Aren't they the loveliest flowers? How many drab spots in our city are made beautiful by their brilliant multi-hued presence! When ripe, Impatiens' pods burst and scatter their seeds, making showy flowerbeds.

Impatience! Not a lovely thing! In the checkout line, in bed waiting for a nurse or just waiting for a red light to turn green, impatience does not create a beautiful scene. Like Impatiens, when our impatience explodes it scatters seeds; however, the seeds of impatience are hurt, anger, and division.

Continuing with the image of flowers, patience tends to be demure—more like Baby's Breath or Statice. Yet, isn't it true that it is the sprig of Baby's Breath that enhances the dozen long-stemmed roses?

Recently, I found a definition for *patience* with a new slant. Rather than describing patience in terms of waiting, this definition said, "Patience is an openness to being present to whatever is."

Living your belief in God's promise to be with you always (and in all ways), it would seem wise just to surrender the day to whatever it brings with that embracing presence.

Reflection

Why not practice that kind of openness—scattering seeds of kindness, understanding, and even pleasant expectation for whatever may unfold? I think you'll find that, like Impatiens, patience spreads.

Pray the Psalms

My lips speak your goodness. Ps 71:15
Bless the Lord, who carries our burdens. Ps 68:20
I offer you a changed heart. Ps 51:19

Giving Spree

Have you noticed the lavish display of color that the trees show in autumn? Flowers, too, favoring the autumn palette, are brilliant reds, yellows, purples, and even metallic shades, like bronze and copper. Autumn is a time when our extravagant God is surely on a giving spree. We pray for eyes to look upon our beautiful world with gratitude and wonder.

There's a story about Dorothy Day that illustrates that kind of giving. The story tells how one morning a generous woman donated a diamond ring to the Catholic Worker House. Immediately, the workers talked of selling the ring and, with the cash from the sale, filling some needs of the poor and also, needs of their mission that had been put on the back burner.

The workers wondered, what would Dorothy Day do with the ring?

That afternoon, Dorothy gave the ring to an elderly poor woman who lived alone and often came to the Catholic Worker for meals.

"The ring would have paid Catholic Workers' rent for most of the year," someone protested. However, Dorothy's response was that the woman had her dignity. She could sell it if she liked and use it for rent money, a trip to the Bahamas, or just keep the ring to admire.

"Do you suppose God created diamonds only for the rich?" remarked Dorothy.

Actually for those who see, God's extravagance is evident at all times.

Reflection

Why not join with God and, in your own way, throwing all measuring to the winds, do some illimitable, off-the-wall, extravagant giving? The ways to do this are themselves limitless and unique. What you do is not as important as that your giving be an "outpouring of the heart" since that kind of loving is the source of God's extravagance.

Pray the Psalms

> God heals the wounded spirit. Ps 34:19
> God fill the earth with love. Ps 33:5

GRATITUDE

Saying your thanks is one way to go. How about letting your words of thanks be made flesh in deeds?

Brother David Steindl-Rast has an insightful slant on the classic view of showing gratitude. He breaks it open, saying, "The root of joy is gratefulness." Brother David maintains, "It is gratitude that makes us joyful."

Let me share a way to increase that joy. Offering your gifts with open hands—no conditions—has a power of enlarging your joy, your peace, and, even, your giving.

I've heard it said many times that others are grateful that our Thanksgiving Day celebrations remain rather free of the commercial trap.

As you plan that celebration, why not include a creative way for your family and friends to thank God? Extend Thanksgiving Day to the entire season, sending personal thank-you notes to people who enrich your life in ways large and small.

Reflection

Accepting the belief that *gratitude* begets *joy*, what happiness awaits you? There are so many areas for beginnings: God's unconditional love, gifts of nature, family, friends, and even disappointments.

Open a door. Send an email. Listen, *really* listen. Offer to help. Stretch your inner self.

Pray the Psalms

> Look to him that you may be radiant with joy. Ps 34:6
> God's love is from all ages. Ps 103:17
> God's love encircles me. Ps 31:22

Ribbons

"I'll tell you how the sun rose—a ribbon at a time."

Those lines from Emily Dickinson's poem, "A Day," are bursting with beauty, theology, and common sense.

If you have ever watched a sunrise, you have an idea of the beauty intimated in the poem. If you have ever experienced the sun rise over Grand Canyon, any description is superfluous.

It seems that God has a way of focusing on *ones*. Scripture reveals this in the story of creation and in stories like the Good Shepherd, who leaves the 99 for the lost **one**.

In Patricia Neunfeldt's "Day's Prayer," we find the same ribbon image:

> "Teach me, O Lord to see that all I need for this day will be provided.
>
> Let me receive it in wonder.
> Wrap it in love.
> Hold it in prayer.
> And return this day to you… gratefully, as gift."
> Amen.

It seems to me that the prayer unravels five ribbons: trust, wonder, love, remembering, and gratitude. Why not focus on one ribbon at a time? Focusing on any *one* ribbon will deepen your appreciation of the gift of a single day. Perhaps too, you will come to know how the Son, so silently, so surely—rises.

Reflection

In another verse, Dickinson describes her awareness of nature as, "That must have been the sun." As you grow in awareness of God's presence in the day's happenings, you might also say, "That must have been the Son." Why not?

Pray the Psalms

Receive each day in wonder.
Let me live in your love. Ps 119:159
Wrap each day in love.
I should give thanks and praise God's name. Ps 69:31
Each night spend some time for saying, "Thanks."
Trust in the Lord. Ps 4:6

Resurrection

The Greek for *resurrection* is a hopeful word. It is translated: "again, standing up." Every spring, we see (really, no need for blind faith) resurrection all around us as the crocuses pop out, the trees bud, and colors intensify.

We hear resurrection in the chirping of the birds and the sounds of children playing. We feel resurrection every time we give in to hope and try once more. Think about it, how do we begin each day? Isn't it "again, standing up?" And if, perchance, we are physically unable to do that, our spirits can still soar.

There is a *power* within us that urges us each morning to embrace life and all its goodness. Seeking that resurrection source, we find that all along it is our God who has been with us. God is the power within—stirring up life, pushing through, helping us to climb out and stand up after every disappointment or seeming defeat.

We seek, but all along Emmanuel is there—God with us always and in all ways—our power for resurrection and life—*if* we open ourselves to him.

Reflection

St. John writes in his prologue: "The Word was God. He was present to God in the beginning. Through him, all things came into being and apart from him nothing came to be. Whatever came to be in him found *life*."

The Psalms express the joy of resurrection. Psalm 118, for example, is that kind of Psalm, affirming a good day with the words, "This is the day the Lord has made;
Let us be glad and rejoice in it!"

Using the ideas from different Psalms, we can deepen our understanding of resurrection and of the Power within us urging us to stand up and... *share*.

Pray the Psalms

Phone a loner.
Look for the face of God. Ps 27:8

Give up your own way.
I call on your name. Ps 116:17

Be Peace.
Be kind to your servant that I may live, that I may keep your word. Ps 119:17

Briefing: Interior Remodeling

Every spring in my childhood home—the inevitable: spring cleaning and interior remodeling!

Scrubbing, repairing, painting, and re-arranging kept our house messy for months.

Baseball proved a big obstacle to progress until my mother's insistence won out, year after year, and my brothers and father were persuaded to help right the chaos. *Spiritual* interior remodeling isn't like that at all. *Spiritual* interior remodeling begins with looking deeper into who I really am, without ties to work or social identity, continuing with prayer and reflection, and culminating in decisive action. The Spirit is the Initiator and Sustainer, promising us a "new heart" and a "new spirit" (Ezekiel 11:19).

The suggestions that follow are meant to lead you to happiness, radiance, and resurrection—a far cry from my childhood memories of chaotic and stress-filled spring cleaning.

Dream Houses

Perhaps you have noticed new houses in your neighborhood. The houses that I've seen lately are like someone's dream come true. Outside, they are large and eye-catching and, I imagine, the inside matches the outside. Sometimes, looking and imagining, I start to wonder what it would be like living inside some of those *dream* houses.

I have a plaque in my kitchen that reads, "Love makes a house a home."

No doubt, it's true that most of us aren't in the market for a new house, but maybe it *is* time for a little *interior* remodeling. Here are some thoughts with accompanying Psalms to get you off to a good start.

Whom do I take for granted? Who in my home could use a little love? "Little" things can make a "big" difference. What little thing can I do—today—to remodel my *home*?

If "love makes a house a home," somehow, love is the answer.

God is Love.

Reflection

God is the energy of new life gracing you each day. (That line, by the way, defines *grace*.) Believe in that limitless grace.

Try some "little" things.

For instance:

> Say, "Thank you," for a special dessert.
> Be forgiving—give a hug.
> *Smile* a welcome home.
> Give special attention.
> Spend some time.
> "Little?" Well, sometimes, it can be a stretch.

Pray the Psalms

> God gives the homeless a home. Ps 68:7
> Find shelter in God. Ps 2:12
> Lord God, all you touch comes alive. Ps 65:12

Doors

Doors are fascinating, aren't they? The poster, "Doors of Dublin," is familiar to many people far beyond the shores of Ireland. Have you seen it? The brightly colored Georgian doors are a symbol of the city. In the eighteenth century, these doors were individually arranged and styled to indicate the grandeur found upon entering the house—the more opulent the entrance, the greater the anticipation of what lay behind the door. Isn't that a fascinating concept?

Perhaps though, the function of doors holds even more interest: "opening to... and closing out...." Metaphorically speaking, we open and close many doors each day. "I can't do that." "I won't do that." "I'll try." "I'd be happy to." "I give up."

The list is endless and clearly points out the power of doors. In fact, it has been said that the doors we open and close each day decide the lives we lead. A thought for musing, isn't it?

In John's gospel, Jesus, "I am the gate, the door." That truth leads us to a understanding of the awesome power that can be ours if we become more aware. Time spent becoming more aware of doors—actual doors and also the figurative ones—promises to be rewarding. Most of all, be mindful that Jesus is the Door opening us to immeasurably more than we can welcome *or* reject.

Reflection

There is one last beautiful analogy between the Doors of Dublin and Jesus, the Door. The Dublin facades were designed to indicate the grandeur to be found within—the more sumptuous the entrance, the greater the anticipation of what lay behind the door. What then can be said about Jesus?

Pray the Psalms

"Lord, summon us into your light." Ps 89:16
Lord, happy those you welcome. Ps 65:5
Open the gates of justice. Ps 118:19

Grooming

Recently, I made a discovery about ducks. Do you know that ducks must coat themselves with special waterproofing oil? Do you know the remarkable thing? This oil is produced beneath their wings. (Who says God doesn't care?)

This natural Creator-initiated procedure is called *grooming*. Ducks must coat themselves with this special oil so that when swimming, they can be *in* yet not *of* the water. Without grooming, ducks sink.

Have you ever felt overwhelmed? Have daily pressures, pains and demands ever given you a *sinking* feeling? Why not try *grooming*? In this instance, grooing means covering yourself with the oil of God's protective presence. How? By calling on God for help, trusting that God will answer you, and then giving thanks for God's response.

Let Psalms 90:12, 105:4, and 50:7 remind you of God's help. The suggestions listed below are ideas for an accompanying action. They are not in order. You can pick and choose:

> Smile.
> Surprise someone.
> Slow down.

Pause: think of how good God is.
Give up your own way.
Share "good news."
Encourage someone.
Be patient.
Do something for the poor.
Listen!
Be available.
Pray for sinners.
Say "yes."
Look with "God's eyes."
Make this day count.

Reflection

Remember the lilies? Not even Solomon in all his splendor was arrayed as these. Would your Creator do less for you? Get *groomed*! Get with it!

Pray the Psalms

The Lord bends down to see heaven and earth. Ps 113:6

You are a people close to the Lord. Ps 148:14

The Lord is near to those who call, to those who cry out from their hearts. Ps 145:18

Meaning and Fulfillment

The daily news can be heavy. September 11, 2001 cloaked our world in reflective seriousness. Hopefully, we also took notice of the many blessings which flow from our extravagant God and received them with deeper gratitude.

One rainy Saturday before September 11, I saw an article on the front page of the *Chicago Tribune* that made my heart happy. The story began with the experience of a young woman in her "quarter-life" crisis. She said, "There are a lot of us asking ourselves what we have gotten out of the last few years. I was writing ads to convince people to buy things they really did not need."

The article continued with similar experiences and awakenings of people in their early and mid-twenties. All were tired of the rat race and were questioning themselves, "What good have I done today?" Gearing their reflections into action, some joined the Peace Corps while others entered helping professions.

Whoa! I'm not recruiting. However, the words "more fulfilling and more meaningful" were dispersed throughout the article, and those two adjectives describe a holy and wholesome life direction for anyone. How about you? Is there some way to try to manifest your gratitude in meaningful ways?

Reflection

God made a beautiful world. Why not pay more attention to it?

Everything that comes to us is a gift. Will you look deeply enough to find the gift?

Try singing or humming throughout the day, a simple melody like "Peace is flowing like a river." Notice if you experience any change in your thoughts or actions.

Pray the Psalms

"Sing to your God, your Savior, your Rock." Ps 5:1

The Lord rules; the earth is eager, joy touches distance lands. Ps 97:1

Give me the life you promise. Ps 119:107

A Clean Heart

Recently, while reflecting on the penitential Psalm 51, I arrived at a wholesome, healing thought. One line of the Psalm reads, "Create a clean heart in me, O God." God creating—not once, but over and over. How awesome!

"God creating." Doesn't that tax the imagination? Just behold the beauty, the detail, and the variety around you. One verse of Psalm 104 vibrates with wonder and praise to this creator God:

> "God, how fertile your genius.
> You shape each thing.
> You fill the world with what you do."

What does it take to believe that God can and, indeed, longs to create a clean heart in each of us?

"Clean" Psalm 51 happens to be a favorite of mine, but for me, the adjective "clean" doesn't quite express it. Looking in the thesaurus, two synonyms completed the metaphor: "wholeness" and "uncluttered." With *wholeness*, I connect to "evolution and transformation"—with *uncluttered*, I add the idea of "free from selfishness".

Reflection

Consider how:

> Love surrendered to the cross so that we might live, and how that same Love continues to re-create our hearts.

The words of Psalm 9:11 then become our own. "Those who know you, trust you; you never desert the faithful."

After this reflection you may want to pray, "Merciful God, I give you my heart—anxious at times, too busy, and self-centered; sometimes unloving and quick to pass judgment. In your own loving and ingenious way, create a clean heart in me."

Pray the Psalms

Restore to us God, the light of your presence, and we shall be saved. Ps 80:4

Gentle is God. Ps 103:13

Bring wisdom to our hearts. Ps 90:12

A Model of Trust

Over the years, an icon pictured in any number of magazines has become sort of a classic. The image is that of a bright yellow dandelion breaking through a crack in the concrete sidewalk.

I'd like to propose that image as a possible model of trust.

Perhaps, there is a difficult project awaiting your efforts. Perhaps, there is a difficult person you encounter every day. Maybe you are in need of a burst of new life. At any rate, maybe this is a sort of *concrete* time in your life.

It seems to me that St. Paul's words to the Romans (Romans 8) are appropriate here.

"We know that the whole of creation has been groaning in labor pains until now (waiting for) the fruits of the Spirit…" "Groaning for wholeness and stretching toward transformation…" describes entering with awareness into the process of evolution.

Keeping the dandelion image in mind and putting your trust in the dandelion's Maker, dare to bloom in unbelievable ways and places.

Reflection

In what ways are you *concrete bound* in your attitude toward:

>Your family responsibilities?
>Your work tasks?
>Your free time?
>Your prayer time?

Remember, Jesus promised that he would send the Holy Spirit. What is impossible for the Spirit?

Pray the Psalms

>Release my cemented heart. Ps 25:17
>The Lord freed me from all my fears. Ps 34:5
>My God, I lean on you. Ps 18:3

Around in Circles

As far back as I can remember "going around in circles" was something to be avoided. However, Christina Baldwin's book, *Calling the Circle*, presented the word in a whole new context: rich with possibilities.

The following quotation from the book is quite lengthy but makes for a soul-satisfying reflection:

> "The sun comes forth and goes down again in a circle. The moon does the same, and both are round. Even the seasons form a great circle in their changing and always come back to where they were. The life of a (person) is a circle from childhood to adulthood, and so it is in everything where power moves,"
>
> —Black Elk.

While still amazed at how inherent the circle is in many areas of life, I providentially came across the words of the poet, Edwin Markham. His lines, I believe, add the *Amen! Alleluia!* to the thoughts of Black Elk.

> "He drew a circle that shut me out...
> But, LOVE and I had the wit to win.
> We drew a circle that took him in."

Reflection

Perhaps the question is: Who needs to be included in your circle?

Pray the Psalms

God's love encircles me. Ps 31:22
Listen today to God's voice. Ps 95:8
Show me your wonderful love. Ps 17:7

With the Spirit

In his book, Gospel Light, John Shea recounts a wonderful story. The story tells about an aging mother who was experiencing a "not untroubled old age."

On the way to a funeral, the mother makes a shocking announcement to her son, "I'm giving up fear."

Shea describes the son as fettered by fears:

> "fear of sickness and death,
> fear of the future,
> fear of losing money and work."

It follows that the son, whose life was unhealthily limited by fear, had doubts about his mother's resolution. However, as the weeks and months passed, his mother proved those doubts to be unfounded. The example of her trust even initiated a noticeable change in the son.

Sounds great, you say, but what about me? You'll find a practical suggestion in Shea's concluding reflection, which is spiced with humor—humor to be taken seriously.

> "Hang around people who are Spirit-filled and releasing Spirit into the world—Spirit is contagious. It blows where it will. Get in the way of the wind."

Reflection

The Israelites are good people to hang with. God was their God. They were His people. The Israelites relied on God's power. They said, "I'm sorry" many times. Most of all, they had great expectations of God on their behalf.

Two suggestions:

Find ways to be your truest, deepest self—what you see is what I am.
Deepen your expectations of God.

Pray the Psalms

You never desert the faithful. Ps 9:11
You cleared away my trouble. Ps 4:2
Let those who trust you be glad. Ps 5:12

Giving Thanks

A friend of mine loaned me a wonderful book—*My Grandfather's Blessings*, by Rachel Naomi Remen, MD. The first chapter is entitled "Receiving Your Blessings" and the author begins,

"Most of us have been given many more blessings than we have received."

Think about that!

The author goes on to say, "We do not take time to be blessed or make space for the blessings."

Is your life so busy, so cluttered, so stuffed with *stuff* that there is not time or space left to receive your blessings? You might want to check this out.

The concept of blessing is bound up with praising and giving thanks—bound up with a way of seeing, understanding, and *being* in our everyday world. We know that God's goodness and love tend us every day. Do you believe that? How so?

Why not take the time to discover *your* many blessings and to make space to receive them, choosing to make each day a day of *thanks-giving*? Each day you meet others with different kinds of hungers. From your abundant gratitude, why not prepare them a *feast*?

Reflection

The great mystic, Meister Eckhart, believed:

> "If the only prayer you ever say in your entire life is 'Thank you,' it will be enough."

Pray the Psalms

All my being, bless the Lord. Ps. 103:1
Goodness and giving fill the days of the just. Ps. 37:26
Graciously, lead me, Lord. Ps. 143:10

Briefing:
A Nothing Day

A nothing day! We've all had them. Days dawn when there is something ahead that we dread, or when our day, seemingly ordinary, brings numerous reversals.

In either case, that is the time for remembering the gift of our extravagant God—grace.

Grace can help us make a nothing day valuable, even shimmering.

The following reflections invite you to consider some simple ways to make each day something special—even, extra special.

Seeking God

"The trick of finding what you didn't lose."

This is a thought from the poet, e.e. cummings. And, what a creative, challenging thought it is, except that, in the case of our God, there is no trick involved.

To prove my point, suppose that you try focusing on finding ways in which God is present in your day. Remember—you will be seeking the God whose name is Emmanuel, God-with-us. You will be seeking a renewed connectedness with God, who said, through Jesus, "I am with you always."

Let the Psalms mark your path, like Psalm 71:3, "(God) to whom I can always turn", or Psalm 66:9 "(God) who kept our spirits alive."

In her book, *Reclaiming the Connections*, Kathleen Fischer confirms that prayer presupposes "that we are in fact always in the presence of God." By trying to be mindful and attentive, you will open yourself to an experience of oneness with God and with the divine in all of life. Of course, you realize that this attentiveness is not of the mind but of the heart.

As you learn to open your heart more and more, you will behold a sense of your dependence on God and your interdependence with others. Then, suddenly, or so it seems, you are responding, discovering, appreciating—yes, even *humming* your praise and gratitude.

Reflection

Since seekers taste the goodness of God, St. Bernard presses further, intimating that finding God leaps beyond our imagining. "I believe though I do not comprehend, and I hold by faith what I cannot grasp with the mind."

Pray the Psalms

God works wonders. Rejoice! Ps 126:3
Let me live in your love. Ps 119:159
I offer myself to you, Lord God. Ps 86:4

Greeting the Risen Christ

The late Bishop Untener of Saginaw tucked a neat idea into one of his books. Recalling the scripture passage about the disciples on the way to Emmaus, he told of how, in some places, an "Emmaus Walk" has become sort of a tradition.

What made this walk different was that the walkers made a point of greeting the people that they met along the way, recognizing that it was by such a greeting that the two disciples on the road to Emmaus met the Risen Christ.

Have you joined in the national pastime? You could greet those you meet on your walk with a "Hi!" or even just a smile. If you're someone who doesn't have the blessing of walking outdoors, why not greet those who happen along in your day?

Either way, try to be aware that you are meeting the *Risen Christ* in that person. You might want to pray the following Psalms:

> The Lord, our God, opens blind eyes. Or change this truth into a request: "Lord God, please open my blind eyes." Ps. 146:8

How can I escape your presence? Ps. 139:7

Reflection

Stretch your faith in the presence of the Risen Lord.

Remember things—and people—aren't always what they seem.

Ask for the grace to be open to the varied presence of Christ. Varied, i.e., people, nature, animals, events both happy and painful.

Pray the Psalms

Let your loveliness shine on us. Ps 90:17

Recount the signs and wonders of God. Ps 105:5

More than wait for the dawn, I watch for the Lord. Ps 130:6

Show Me

"Now" is the moment. Psalm 65:2

In his gospel, John pictures the resurrection breakfast scene where Jesus asks Peter; "Do you love me?" Jesus added three times, "Show me!"

Remember the song from *My Fair Lady*? "Don't talk of stars burning above. If you're in love, show me!"

Can you hear God saying that to you? God, challenging you, saying, "I love you, and I believe you, but how about showing me that you love Me?"

"How?" you ask.

Here are a few suggestions:

- Consider your part in environmental preservation.
- Send a card or *read* to someone.
- Let go of some security—a possession, a place, a pleasure.
- Surprise someone who's ill.

Reflection

"Let go"—discover how you are more than your possessions.

Earth is a gift. Unpack the meaning of "sustainability."

Where there is no life, put life.

Pray the Psalms

One thing I seek: to be caught up in God's beauty. Ps 27:4

Favor me with your love. Ps 69:14

See the wonders God does across the earth. Ps 46:9

Glimpses of God

I recently treated myself to a wonderfully nourishing book, *Glimpses of Grace*.

The book is a collection of daily reflections from the extensive writings of Madeline L'Engle.

One selection is a true story about Psalm 23. It tells how the English often entertain guests after dinner by inviting them to share their talents by singing or reciting. At one such party, Charles Laughton recited Psalm 23. He was applauded loudly for his magnificent performance.

At the same party, a very elderly aunt, being both deaf and drowsy, missed his great performance. Later on, the guests coaxed her into reciting something. In a quivery voice she also did the twenty-third Psalm. However, tearful emotion muted the response of her listeners.

One of the guests made mention of this to the famous actor, "You recited that Psalm absolutely superbly. It was incomparable. So why were we so moved by that funny little old lady?"

He replied, "I know the Psalm. She knows the Shepherd."

This story could be a springboard for your Psalm prayer, could deepen your desire to know the Shepherd.

The Psalms image God in different ways: loving caretaker, patient listener, unending light, steady rock, immeasurable joy—and many, many more. Do you have a Psalm that expresses the way you presently know God? If not, for starters, you might try Ps 104:34 or Ps 18:29. They are meant to urge you to search for images that invite you to experience God in a *new* way.

Reflection

Remember: God is new every day. Who helps you walk in God's presence?

Ask for a deeper awareness of how God wants to be present in your day. And don't forget to listen.

Try to remember a thought from Psalm 23 throughout this day.

Share something from your full cup.

Pray the Psalms

Your mercy spans the sky. Ps 36:6
You crown the year with riches. Ps 65:12
You heal the wounded spirit. Ps 34:19

Extraordinary Time

Most of the year, we rush and fuss to keep on schedule. Then comes summer. God, in his illimitable way, bowls us over with long sunny days, birds' song, and fields of flowers. The livin' is easy. We slow up. We unwind. We lighten up.

The church calendar designates the summer months as *ordinary time*. I see them as *extra-ordinary time*. Why? Because having enough time and a place to simply *be* does wonders for our prayer.

Theologian, author Michael Quoist says it well, "Prayer is not so much a matter of straining out toward God as it is relaxing before God." The weather, the environment, our attitude—all that is summertime, as we know it—can gift us with graced moments.

Our God is a playful God. Proverbs makes this observation, which John in his gospel applies to Jesus abiding in the Father.

> "I was beside him as his craftsman.
> And I was his delight day by day.
> Playing before him all the while,
> Playing on the surface of the earth."

Choose a Psalm or two that awakens in you a sense of JOY for nothing in general, and just everything in particular—especially, an awareness of our extravagant, loving God.

Reflection

Remember God's promises are honey sweet. Ps 119:103
Who shines love on us each dawn?
Who is our sun—our shield?
Whose mercy spans the sky?

Pray the Psalms

You give me rest in green meadows. Ps 23:2
God owns this planet and all its riches. Ps 24:1
Come see God's wonders. Ps 66:5

God's Energy

The enduring truth is that God so loved us that he gave us his only Son. Why? That we may have life—life to the full. In 1 John 5, we learn that, "Whoever possesses the Son possesses life."

Some see life as a reflection of God's energy. St. Thomas Aquinas assures us that our source of life is within. Think of it: your life—energized by God's energy.

What is life for you? And, more importantly, what is this life that comes when we possess Jesus?

Prayer, particularly the Psalms, coaxes us to discover the answers to these questions. Psalm 13:7 proclaims "I will sing to the Lord, who treats me with kindness." And how about Psalm 104:34? It reads, "Let my song give joy to God who is a joy to me."

Each day, why not ask for an awareness of life around you? Rejoice when you recognize a sign of life in a smile, a budding leaf, a phone call, or a sudden inspiration (movement of life from within). Try sharing that spark of life with someone. You might even want to record the signs of life that you have received and shared. Such a practice promises a wonderful awakening to the Living God.

Reflection

Lift someone's spirit today.
A smile is a beautiful sign of life—share a smile.
Thank God for your energy throughout today

Pray the Psalms

Nourish our joy. Ps 85:7
You show me the road to life. Ps 16:11
Your goodness is boundless. Ps 71:19

An Awesome Day

"Have a nice day." How does that make you feel? Does it register any feeling in you at all?

No doubt about it, the expression is well-meant, but it is also threadbare. My private confession, now made public, is, "I'm sick of it." It is a string of empty words.

What I want is:

- An awesome day!
- A loving day!
- A graced day!

The poet e.e. cummings says,

> "when every leaf opens without any sound… when more than was lost has been found, has been found and having is giving and giving is living—… it's spring (all our night becomes day) o, it's spring!"

It is spring when nature blooms bright and bold. It is spring whenever we live and believe that resurrection is ours, because scripture does not attest to something that happened long ago. It proclaims something that can happen—now—to us.

I can be blind to God's beauty that surrounds me or—I can open my eyes to the wonder. I can bury myself in misery or—I can reach out to others with a smile. I can breed anger or—I can nurture peace.

Reflection

Many Psalm verses reflect what it is like to be a resurrection person. I'll bet you will be surprised to see how many describe *you*. Here's one that resonates with me, "When help comes to me, joy fills my heart. I thank God in song" (Ps 28:7).

Pray the Psalms

Ask to see with God's eyes. Shout joy to the Lord. Ps 33:1

Before retiring, take a look at the night sky. Release my trapped heart. Ps 25:17

Help someone grow in his relationship with God. Delight in the Lord who satisfies your heart. Ps 37:4

The Way of Love

During the fourth century, Christians began to make pilgrimages to the Holy Land. There, they walked the path that Jesus was believed to have walked as he carried his cross through the streets of Jerusalem. They called this prayer-walk "The Way of the Cross," though "The Way of Love" would also have described it well. By the eleventh century, the Christians had built tableaux representing these stations in their homelands.

Think about it: isn't there a pattern to most of your days? Isn't your time spent in mostly the same places, with the same people? Your day has a certain number of *stations*, too.

Recently, I discovered a more inviting definition for the Lenten word *repent*. According to this definition, "to repent means to re-think, to make things new by receiving them for what they are—God's gifts."

So, you can begin the day as you usually do, fed by the radio, TV news, traffic and weather reports, and accounts of the most recent crime; or, you can *repent/re-think* beginning each day more aware of God's presence.

Reflection

This, of course, is a beautiful way—not easy, but beautiful—for you to live out the spirit of repentance and to make a new Way of the Cross. By living out that definition in those places and with those persons who are your daily "*stations*," your days will become a real "Way of Love."

Pray the Psalms

> Show me your wonderful love. Ps 17:7
> Teach me your ways. Ps 119:26
> Teach us to make use of our days. Ps 90:12

Turn Your Thoughts

Turn your clock ahead—*spring forward*. You've probably done that many times. Turning clocks ahead signals the future—good things of spring and summer. Psalm 63 says it rightly, "I feast at your rich table."

We eagerly seek a glimpse of spring's first flower. We discover tiny buds on a wintry brown tree. Buried seeds spring up, greening and growing. We look forward to grass, sunshine, and the lake warm enough for swimming. We know that summer days will be long enough and light enough for picnics, play, and lawn concerts.

Though I don't remember the entire song, this one line from Roger's and Hammerstein's movie, *Flower Drum Song*, is inspirational enough:

"A hundred thousand miracles are happening every day."

Just look to Nature to see these wondrous miracles. Nature *enfolds*. One definition for *enfolds* is *embraces*. Think of it being embraced by nature gently, spontaneously. Taking miracles for granted becomes easy, doesn't it?

Amazingly, taking others—even God—for granted is just as easy.

Reflection

Perhaps then, while you turn your clock ahead, you might turn your thoughts to how you can grow in appreciation for the wonderful gifts in your life.

Pray the Psalms

Stretch toward heaven, open high and wide. Ps 24:7
Hold dear all God's gifts. Ps 103:2
I know your love is unending. Ps 89:3

Waking Up Happy

Someone asked, "What makes the soul wake up so happy?"

That *is* something worth thinking about. Keep in mind, too that a beautiful question deserves a beautiful answer.

Perhaps it would help to phrase the question more specifically. What makes *your* soul wake up so happy? I'm certain that your answer will be as individual as you are.

However, here are a few thoughts for starters:

> You're ready for all the possibilities of a brand new day.
>
> The darkness of night has slipped away.
>
> The God of Light has come brightening the day, enkindling your spirit.
>
> Outdoors, nature is waiting to share color, sounds, and healing silence.
>
> As Psalm 63 suggests, "You feast at a rich table."
>
> Wonderful people enrich your life beyond measure.

And wonder of wonders, God has promised to be with you always—and in all ways.

Reflection

Poet Jessica Powers reflects, "God within me stoops to sharing the splendor that is His alone."

What makes *your* soul wake up so happy? Why not pray about the answer? Here's one clue: The Lord pours out riches. Ps 85:13

Pray the Psalms

Your love is better than life. Ps 63:4

Lord, your name is our joy, and your justice, our strength. Ps 89:17

You nourish the earth with what you create. Ps 104:13

Forever Love

Sometimes, I wonder why June is the chosen month for celebrations. Weddings, graduations, and reunions seem to abound in June. Because of them, June sparkles with excitement and joy.

However, in Psalm 118, there are two jewels of verse that open wide all twelve months, all 365 days, to celebration. The first is:

> "This is the day which the Lord has made.
> Let us be glad and rejoice."

Try focusing on: *which the Lord has made*. Doesn't that phrase hold more specialness than we could ask for or imagine?

Add to that wonder the truth that **every** day is the Lord's creation. Why shouldn't, why *wouldn't* we rejoice? Why not then, begin each morning with the thought:

"*This* is the day *which the Lord has made*." So, how will I spend it?

Are you ready to consider the awesome source of each day's reason for celebration? That source is found in the other line from Psalm 118. It is a line that is so succinct and so true: "God's love is forever."

Now on occasion, there may be some stormy weather, but God's eternal love can never be rained out. That's God's promise. That eternal love is mine to have; yet, that love is also meant to be shared. The marvelous part is that the sharing will leave me with more to give, more joy, more desiring.

Reflection

Each day—this day—*every* day is "the day which the Lord has made. Be glad and rejoice!"
Make a change today.
Mend something broken.
Be a blessing.

Pray the Psalms

God works wonders. Ps 126:3
You show me the road to life. Ps 16:11
My soul lives for the Lord! Ps 22:31

Beauty in the Ordinary

"God is the beauty in all things beautiful."

It must have been October when St. Augustine wrote that. Who but God could lavish such awesome color, such sumptuous beauty, as the trees adorned in autumn splendor?

Another saint, John of the Cross, offers us a different awareness of God's beauty. John's insight is this: "The beauty of the Lord lies in its willing confinement in the ordinary."

"Willing confinement in the ordinary." Different, isn't it? Different from what we see and hear on television. Different from magazine ads that promise "holistic beauty from head to toe" in the use of anything from hair coloring to cereal.

Think about it. "The beauty of the Lord lies in its willing confinement in the ordinary."

Scriptures unfold a number of such scenes:

- Jesus blessing the little children
- Jesus waiting on the shore for the apostles with breakfast prepared
- Jesus washing the feet of the apostles—to mention a few.

Who or what would you name *ordinary* in your day?

Surprising, isn't it what fills your minutes, your hours, your day, your life? Just think how you could beautify each day for others, and for yourself.

Reflection

Why not *seek for, find in, and add to* the beauty in the ordinary of each day? Next to that beauty, wouldn't scarlet maples pale?

Pray the Psalms

May I live to praise You. Ps 119:175
God turns the dry land into fertile valleys. Ps 107:35
Look always for the presence of God. Ps 105:4

Briefing: Soul Music

"If God is Lord of heaven and earth, how can I keep from singing?"

Remember that Quaker song which so simply states such a profound truth?

That truth believed and lived would comfort us in sorrow and coax us to dance in joy. Knowing that music is the language of the soul, and that to sing is to pray twice, the reflections that follow encourage us to use sacred and popular music in prayer.

Singing the Psalms

While shopping at Ace Hardware the other day, I heard the checkout girl singing softly. I remarked that something good must have happened. Smiling, she replied, "I'm just happy." That was obvious.

As I left the store, I heard the other checkout girl joining in the song. Returning to my car, I began to sing because, as you know, singng is contagious. One can't stay crabby and sing.

On the merit of singing, Oliver Wendell Holmes observes, "Alas! For those who never sing but die with all their music in them."

You know, of course, that a Psalm is a song but have you ever noticed how often the word *sing* appears in the Psalms? See Psalms 42:10, 89:2, and 47:7 for starters. May one conclude that ours is a happy God who created us to be happy, too?

Remember that Perry Como favorite that could coax a song from a frog and, at the same time, give answer to the usual excuse, "I can't?" The beginning of the song goes like this:

> "Sing! Sing a song!
> Sing out loud.
> Sing out strong."

Reflection

Remember, to sing is to pray twice. Why not try singing a prayer?

> "God wrote a lovely song
> when He made you.
> May you continue to be
> music to His ears
> every day of your life
> and for all eternity."
>
> —Author Unknown

Pray the Psalms

Awake my soul to song. Ps 57:9

A new song for the Lord! Sing it and bless God's name. Ps 96:1

Come sing with joy to God. Ps.95:1

Remember

The account of the disciples on the road to Emmaus is a familiar Easter gospel story. One month, *National Catholic Reporter* featured a copy of George Roualt's etching, *Christ and the Two Disciples on the Way to Emmaus* with the title line: "The Road to Emmaus passes through every town."

It is easy to identify with that line because, in fact, the disciples' fear and disillusionment, maybe even their running away from a problem, is a very human experience.

Recalling Luke's story and reflecting on it, we, too, know the jolt of high hopes to low reality. Have we perhaps also trudged along, not seeing that we have the keys to our own solutions, in plain sight? The Risen Christ remains a stranger because our focus is on the negative? If we simply look up and *see*, we realize that He is there, with us.

It would seem that Emmaus could occur in the steps of an ordinary day. The key is awareness and conviction that Christ gifts us with His presence in many different ways—simple ways. Some we catch, some we miss.

Marty Haugen gives a clue in his song, "We Remember," using such examples as

bread and faces when he wrote, "See the face of Christ revealed in every person standing by your side."

I find a short request during my morning prayer helpful.

"Open my eyes, Lord, to see as you see."

Reflection

As you remember _____
Celebrate by _____
Show your believing by _____

Pray the Psalms

Shout for joy to God. Ps 47:2
My whole life give praise! Ps 146:2

An Artist of Being

My parents were right when they said that one day I'd regret not pursuing my music lessons. Among other things, it meant missing some precious living and giving. Can the joy created by music be measured? Who can account for the spirit a song may resurrect?

I'm sure that you have had such musical experiences, and maybe even had regrets like mine. However, there is hope for those who claim no artistic gifts. I found inspiration and encouragement in an article on talent.

"No need to use brush, clay, or guitar," the article proposed. "Let life itself be your medium—become an artist of being."

It seems to me that nature can teach us some lessons on the art of being. What do birds do best? What about stars? And flowers? In their singing, in their shining, and in their blooming beauty, by reflecting what their Creator made them to be, they all attest to the glory of God.

Reflection

Any time is the right time for coming *alive*. Why not join nature in living life to the fullest—in sharing yourself? And we have help: "I have come that you may have life—life to the full." (John 10:10)

Remembering that the Giver of that promise can be trusted, why not try to be alive and to share that life?

Pray the Psalms

All the earth sings to you, sings to your name. Ps 66:4
All day I sing your glory. Ps 71:8
Make music and sing the Lord's mighty wonders. Ps 105:2

Bustin'

"June is bustin' out all over." This old song, from Rodgers and Hammerstein's *Carousel*, can still call forth contagious joy and new energies.

God began it all. Genesis tells it with thrilling antitheses:

- light from darkness
- water and dry land
- birds, swimming creatures, and land animals

God decorated the sky with the sun, moon and stars. God softened the dry earth and colored it with flowers, fruits, vegetables, and seasonal growth. All God made is good. So it is.

Remembering, too, that God is at the heart of our evolving universe, we realize that Love is life's energy.

The Trinity reveals God as Love.

In her book, *The Unbearable Wholeness of Being*, Ilia Delio expands the belief in the new Genesis, "This dynamic personal relatedness of infinite love means that creation is not a mere external act of God, an object on the fringe of divine power; rather, it emerges out of the innermost depths of Trinitarian life."

Let that goodness call forth in you contagious joy and new energies.

Reflection

O God of too much giving, with heartfelt gratitude, let me enjoy each day. Let me touch, hear, smell, taste, and see that you are good. This is *my* song…! (The completion is yours!)

Pray the Psalms

>Turn to God, be bright with Joy. Ps 34:6
>Drink in the richness of God. Ps 34:9

God's Love

Love has as many expressions as there are personalities. Flowers, jewelry, and poetry are three traditional ways to show love… and then there are songs.

Love songs run the gamut from pathetically sad to ridiculously exaggerated to sublimely beautiful. They can be powerful reminders of our restless hearts, which St. Augustine said could only be at rest in God. Here are lines from Psalms that focus on God's extravagant, unconditional love:

> God's love encircles me like a protecting wall (Ps 31:22).
> God's love is forever (Ps 136:2).
> The Lord pours out his riches (Ps 85:13).

As a wise youngest sister, I could always tell if my brothers were happily in love. They warbled like canaries! Are you ever so happy that you can't keep from singing?

I would like to make a suggestion beyond praying and singing the Psalms. Why not make up your own love songs to that God who loved you into being?

I often make parodies from familiar songs. Here's one I made to the tune of the Mary Tyler Moore's theme song:

You turn my world on, Lord
Because you're near.
You take a nothing day
And make it rare and dear.
Love is all around us;
So, why worry?
You lift us in tender mercy
We're goin' to make it.
And how!

Reflection

Singing makes us contagiously happy—like being in love.

Since God is Lord of heaven and earth, how can we keep from singing?

Pray the Psalms

I dance for joy at your constant love. Ps 31:8

I will sing to my God, make music for the Lord. Ps 104:33

Let my song give joy to God, who is a joy to me. Ps 104:34

Songs of Love

Have you ever been listening to a song you've heard hundreds of times, and suddenly it is as if you are hearing it for the first time? The "same old thing" instantly transforms into a new message.

That happened to me recently. The song, "Perhaps Love," with Placido Domingo and John Denver, was playing in the background. Suddenly, I *really* heard the lyrics. Reflecting on them, it became clear to me that, almost line for line, the song images are also the scriptural images for *love*, for the way God loves you and me.

> "Perhaps love is like a resting place
> A shelter from the storm
> It exists to give you comfort
> It is there to keep you warm
> And in those times of trouble
> When you are most alone
> The memory of love will bring you home."

John's gospel could be summarized in one word: *LOVE*. In particular, the Last Supper discourses promise *forever* love.

"I will not leave you orphans; I will come to you." John 14:18

"I will come back again and talk you to myself so that where I am, you also may be." John 14:3
"Remain in me, as I remain in you." John 15:4
"I have called you *friends*." John 15:15

Long before John Denver's song, scripture offered similar metaphors for Jesus.

Gate John 10:9 In the Good Shepherd scene, Jesus is the entry gate for the sheep just as He is the way for us.
Light John 9:5
Dwelling Place John 1:14
Life John 14:6
Bread John 6:35

Try recalling other examples from scripture and from your own experience that fit the song's images.

Reflection

Why not try a second listening to *the same old thing?* Then, like the last lines of Denver's song, your listening will hold new meaning for you.

> "If I should live forever
> And all my dreams come true
> My memories of love will be of you"
>
> —*(My God!)*

Pray the Psalms

Lord God, your love is better than life. Ps 63:4
Your goodness and love tend me every day of my life. Ps 23:6
Your ways are my song. Ps 119:54

A Real Promise

Rarely, no, never, do I welcome that day of the month when I take care of bills. However, a graphic of a phone cord in my electric bill proved an exception. Right off, it reminded me of who makes my day, who keeps me going, trying, stretching.

Jesus is our Connection, our Power.

A song by James E. Moore began humming inside me. Perhaps you know it:

> "I will be with you.
> That is my promise.
> I will be with you forever more.
> Trust in my love. Bring me all your cares for I will
> be with you forever more."

The verse gives us further assurance:

> "You are my people and I am your God.
> I made a promise to be with you always
> because I really love you."

Wonderful as it sounds, this is more than a song. It is a real promise that can be found at the end of Matthew's gospel where Jesus says, "And know that I am with you until the end of the [world]." (Mt. 28:20)

John's gospel uses the metaphor of the vine and the branches to describe this connection and the power that becomes ours through communion with Jesus. Psalm 80:15-16 proclaims, "Turn our way, God of might, look down from heaven; tend this vine you planted—cherish it once more."

Reflection

As we continue to believe and to act on Jesus' promise, the words become flesh. We might find ourselves stretched beyond our usual responses with a song in our hearts.

Pray the Psalms

Praise the Lord of Goodness, the God of lasting love! Ps 106:1

I know your love is unending, your fidelity outlasts the heavens. Ps 89:3

Beautiful Noise

We're in the section entitled "Soul Music". Are you wondering what *noise* is doing here- and *beautiful* at that?

For me, it began when Neil Diamond's song, "Beautiful Noise" popped into my head and slid into my whole being, proving again just how contagious melodies can be.

The lyrics tell of the music of life: life's music unfolding in joy and discord. Do you remember that melody? The song is engaging with a contagios beat. The lyrics, too, are intriguing and lead to thoughts and questions about life and its gifts.

Early in my life, I would definitely have categorized hard times with noise. In later years, with reading and reflection, I have come to value *darkness,* and the *noises* of every day that are not immediately identifiable as music. To believe Isaiah, "I will give you the treasures of darkness and riches hidden in secret places so that you may know that it is I, God…, who calls you by name." Is. 45:3

Listen! What are the sounds of life *within* you? When was the last time you listened to them?

Think of how Jesus opened a world of sounds for the deaf man. (Mark 7: 31-37) Why not ask for a similar gift for yourself—to be more open to the God-sounds in your life?

Reflection

What is that beautiful noise beggin' from you?
Thank you? I'm sorry? Welcome? I love you?

Pray the Psalms

I set my insight to music. Ps 49:5
You drilled ears for me to hear. Ps 40:7
Fill me with happy songs. Ps 51:10

Knocking at the Door

Throughout the gospels, Jesus' love is expressed in an invitation to come closer, to discover what the eye has not seen, what the ear has not heard nor can be imagined, and to all that God's love has prepared. The Book of Revelation gives us another example in the scene where Jesus knocks at the door and, if it is opened, He intends to go inside for an intimate meal (3:20).

One of my three cookbooks is titled "Cooking with Love." I'm not certain just why I keep it. The recipes aren't that savory. One thing for sure, the title always reminds me to do what it says—cook with love. As I do that, I find I'm more careful, more reflective, and more intentional. I remember Jesus saying that what you do for the least, you do for me. (Matthew 25:40)

What a creative spin on prayer and presence.

Reflection

The awesome thing is that God continues to knock at the door of our hearts. Each time is another opportunity to be more loving—to invite Him in and share your meal.

Who needs your open door?

How do you invite someone in?

Pray the Psalms

The Lord will give you power. Ps 37:34

Now is the moment. Ps 65:2

God's Song

Song has flowed into these Spirit Script pages. This time let us reflect on "God's song."

No doubt, you are familiar with "The Song of Songs" in the Old Testament. In exquisite, lyric form, the poet expressed God's love for His people, us, you. God, of course, is the Lover while you are the Beloved.

Imagine then, God singing this to you, "Arise, my Beloved, my beautiful one, and come!" (Song of Songs 2:10)

Creation is God's overture, an overture that continues to send melody into our everyday. In an ordinary day, for example, we might hear the song of birds, the solo of the wind, rippling brooks, and maybe the woodpecker's beat. Haven't you also, at one time or another, been soothed by the lazy lapping of waves?

What a wondrous thought that our Creator God not only dazzled us with a world of color, but also wooed us with sound. Think of it, all the lovely music that has ever caressed your spirit had its beginnings in the airwaves.

A voice to sing is truly a gift of God. To sing is to pray twice.

Know what's most encouraging about God's listening? God's always tuned to station L.O.V.E., even if your signal isn't always strong, or your transmission is a little off-key.

Reflection

Isaiah knew the lyrics to God's song that through many variations remains a love song, "You are precious in my eyes. I love you" (Isaiah 43:4).

As you listen and become more attuned, what does God's song bring forth in you? Awe? Joy? Gratitude? Wonder? Compassion?

Pray the Psalms

Let all who seek you and count on your strength sing and dance and cheer "Glory to God." Ps 40:17

Our hearts find joy in the Lord, we trust God's holy name. Ps 33:21

Sending the Best

"When you care enough to send the very best." Whether or not everyone believes in that commercial, everyone knows it's the slogan for Hallmark greeting cards. You can even peek on the back of the card just to be sure the sender cares enough. I've found a fresh way of sending the best to *the BEST*—our God.

How about a song? If not out loud, how about a song in your heart? In fact, that is where the real music starts. I'm thinking of all kinds of songs. The best ones not only have haunting melodies but also lyrics that are timeless. Remember the theme from the Mary Tyler Moore show, "Who can take a nothing day and suddenly make it all seem worthwhile"?

Have you ever faced a day with dread? Have you ever been tempted to call in sick to avoid an unpleasant situation?

Have you ever tried a better way, in fact, the best?

The Psalms, song, poetry, prayer lead us to melody. Psalm 104 says,

> "I will sing to my God,
> make music for the Lord as long as I live.
> Let my song give joy to God, who is a joy to me."

Reflection

Recently, I happened upon some poems from the Hindu poet, Tagore. Here are a few lines that I hope will encourage you to put a song in your heart:

> "With songs I search for you all around me and in my mind, every day of my life.
> Songs taught me so much and have shown me so many paths.
> Songs have discovered for me so many stars in the sky of my heart.
> They have led me to a colorful land of joys and sorrows through a land full of mysteries." …

So sing! Sing a song!

Pray the Psalms

I sing to you, my God, my strong tower of safety. Ps 59:18
Sing God a new song. Ps 33:3

Love's Lesson

Your disciples slept,
I never entered
your Gethsemane—
agony garden.
Your garden scared me.

One day, you opened
Love's own mystery.
Listening, I learned.
My focus changed from
suffering to love.

'Tis the Season

Briefing:
'Tis the Season

If, as Thomas Merton writes, "The desire to find God and to see Him and to love Him is the one thing that matters," and if all longings are really longings for God; then, all time is God-time. God is for all seasons. In the liturgical seasons, as celebrated by the Church, we are directed to focus on particular aspects of Jesus' life, which, in turn, freshen our search, and encourage our perseverance.

Spirit Scripts' *Tis the Season* invites you to do just that.

Becoming New

What do we mean when we say, "Happy New Year?" *Webster's New Collegiate Dictionary* defines "new" as, "being other than the former or old."

Perhaps there's a piece of this definition in our wish. We're hoping, for example, that last year's failures and pain are in the past. Speaking through the prophet Isaiah, God says,

> "Remember not the events of the past, the things of long ago, consider not." Isaiah 43:18

The dictionary says "new" also means: "becoming fresh." Becoming fresh! How inviting!

Remember what the priest poet, Gerard Manley Hopkins wrote about freshness, "There lives the dearest freshness deep down things."

Deep down, deep *within* is where freshness is found. It is where God is.

Instead of making the usual New Year's resolutions, which we hope will change us without too much effort, the Holy Spirit urges us to give ourselves to God who promises, "I create life to be a joy, and you to be a delight." (Isaiah 65:18)

Believing in this God of Freshness, we can break out of our mold. We can ask, "Creator, reshape my heart" (Ps 51:12). Each day will be new with possibilities. Believe it!

This is what God means by Happy New Year.

Reflection

There are many ways to change. Here are a few suggestions:

Make a fresh start to the way you begin your day:

- In a relationship that needs healing;
- In the way you listen;
- In giving others a chance.

Pray the Psalms

You <u>never</u> desert the faithful. Ps 9:11
Trust God. Be at peace. Ps 37:3

Keeping Christmas Alive

The practice of keeping the Christmas spirit alive all year has been promoted in different ways and at different times. This poem by Jim Strathdee is convincing:

> When the song of the angels is stilled,
> When the star in the sky is gone,
> When the Magi have found their way home,
> The work of Christmas begins....

The poet then lists some of the works of tender mercy and some ways to approach God's creation with gratitude. The idea seemed so Spirit-filled, I said, "Why not?"

Here are five suggestions for keeping Christmas alive.

- To see God's people everywhere. And so to welcome them.
- To bring joy to each day. Run with this, the possibilities are countless.
- To make music in someone's heart. A voice isn't needed—only the desire.
- To heal a broken soul with love: Prayer is healing. Words can be healing. What do you find healing?
- Strathdee writes: "To feel the earth below, the sky above."

- What "wonder"—full way could you lift your spirit to the sky?

Reflection

Day-to-day, the Psalms remind us that God is our partner, cheering us on with gifts of grace. "You show me the road to life; boundless joy at your side forever" (Ps. 16:11).

Who knows? This might turn out to be the longest Christmas ever. Go for it!

Pray the Psalms

> Let your faithful ones bless you. Ps 145:10
> They are wise who depend on God. Ps 146:5

Give Thanks

Midway into Lent, the message on a scrap of paper in my Psalm book reads, "Instead of sacrifice, give thanks" (Ps 50:14).

Though most of us associate Lent with sacrifice, I invite you to try to go through a Lenten season while living this Psalm line, "Instead of sacrifice, give thanks."

Think about it for a minute. What do you suppose might happen if you made a deliberate effort to say "thanks" to God for the happenings of each day as they occur?

- Would you slip out of the spirit of Lent?
- Would it create a spirited family table?
- Would it nourish your relationship with others?
- Would it color a "red" tension in pastel shades?
- Would the meaning of Lent change for you?

Why not try and find out?
"Instead of sacrifice, give thanks."

Reflection

As you know, besides words, there are countless ways of saying, "Thank you."

Re-think Lent as a giving time—not particularly a giving-up time. Let your own creativity inspire you.

What if on awakening and just before retiring, you prayed a "Thanks be to God"?

Pray the Psalms

With a heart full of thanksgiving, I proclaim Your wonders, Lord. Ps 9:2

I profess You are my Lord, my greatest good. Ps 16:2

Springtime in December

Are you, like so many others, ready for spring in December? Remember those mornings when snowfall replaces sunrise, when all cars are salted gray, when looking out the window is as far as you could or would go? Forget those days. **Let's be grateful!**

If the anticipation of the coming holidays has begun to weigh you down, substitute a *gratitude list* instead of a Christmas list.

> "A new world of wonders! The Lord is with us" (Ps 126:2).

> Let's remember those poetic lines from John's gospel, "God so loved the world that he gave his only Son...." The Incarnation made this unbelievable gift clear: God wants to be with us.

Paula D'Arcy says it simply, "God comes to you disguised as your life." God is hidden and revealed in your day. Everything can lead you to God, everything—even the holiday rush or the weather.

For example, I smile every time I remember the scene a friend of mine's grandson created during a pre-Christmas Saturday at the grocery store. On entering, he noticed a tired, crabby clerk. Snuggling up, he asked, "How about a little Christmas Spirit?"

Reflection

Think about that, and as you do, the following suggestion might be helpful. Use the phrase, "God so loved *the world* that…", changing the word "world" to "me". "God so loved *me*…."

Then, see what happens.

Pray the Psalms

Celebrate God's love. Ps 107:8
Lord, you give from your goodness. Ps 119:68

Meetings

Let's begin with a couple of thoughts that I hope will stretch to a new meaning for us.

- First thought: Pentecost celebrates the outpouring of the Holy Spirit.
- Second thought: The first Pentecost happened at a meeting.

This second thought led theologian Ronald Rolheiser to muse, "When they write our history, they'll simply say, 'They met a lot.'" How true!

Rolheiser was referring to formal, call-to-order meetings; however, what if we considered a different meaning of the word, "meeting"? Consider the line, "How many people will you be meeting today?"

As Christians, we believe that the Spirit of God dwells within us (1 Cor 3:16). The ways that we welcome and respond to each other mirrors our response to God (Mt 10:10).

The people of India have a beautiful way of putting this belief into practice. On meeting even a total stranger they bow and say, "Namaste," which means, "I greet the divine spark within you."

Since we do *this kind* of meeting a lot, why not let these reflections on the Spirit's indwelling and on Pentecost help us to focus on the graced experience of our meeting and greeting those we encounter each day?

Reflection

Acknowledging the Spirit dwelling within another strengthens the spark of God in that person. It also increases the awareness of God in us.

Pray the Psalms

"Lord, show me the way." Ps 25:4
I walk with you, God, in the light of your life. Ps 56:14

Sounds of Summer

It's summer—summer, a time when we let more of the outside in. Birds are singing. Crickets are chirping. Dogs are yapping. We hear the whirring of lawn mowers, voices of all ages, and the occasional *whack* of a tennis ball hitting a racket.

The sounds of summer have a way of connecting us with life. If we try, they can also connect us with the *God of Life*. Psalm 46 gives us a clue, "Be still and know that I am God."

Consider this possibility: Welcome those summer sounds—a beautiful noise.

Then, be still for a second, praising the *Living God*. "Celebrate God's love, in such abundance, all the wonders revealed" (Ps 107:15).

Consider too, summer's abundance. It has a way of increasing our awareness of Jesus' promise, "I have come that you may have life—life to the full."

The abundance of summer fulfills that promise. Try shifting your consciousness from distractions (television, personal problems, or other people's drama) and just look—really *look* at God's extravagant beauty that surrounds you. This beauty enters through your eyes, but it can only be perceived through the heart.

Be still. Ask for the gift.

Reflection

Why not try opening the window of your heart?
Why not plan each day to give a few minutes just being with nature?

Pray the Psalms

I rejoice before you, Lord, let your word bring me light. Ps 119:169
Smile upon me and teach me your ways. Ps 119:135

Shouting for Joy

Shouting for joy sums up the Psalms of praise and, believe it or not, it is this category of Psalms that we can live out, especially in autumn.

Think about it. Isn't autumn a time

- When we seize every opportunity for a last hurrah to summer
- When the start of a new season invites us to begin again
- When the dazzling colors of nature awaken us to God's presence waiting to be discovered in the who, what, and why of our day
- When the richness of nature's striking changes assures us that God's gifts exceed all that we need for spiritual growth
- When, without a doubt, we are called to enter into life *as it is*, shouting for joy!

Reflection

In the Psalms, we meet challenge, tender mercy, and new life. Though some Psalms focus on sin, sorrow, and even revenge, many Psalm lines are bursting with praise. So ecstatic is the Psalmist's wonder at times that we are invited to reach the heavens. Lines of praise tell of the wondrous, beautiful, bountiful presence of a caring God who calls us out of our darkness into God's radiant light. Why not let autumn and the Psalms remind us of our own place in God's plan?

Why not let it be a time to open our eyes, our ears, and our hearts—not listlessly, not cautiously, but with spirit and *shouting for joy*?

"I dance for joy at your constant love," proclaims Psalm 31 and Psalm 23 declares, "My cup is more than full."

Pray the Psalms

> You fill the world with awe. Ps 104:1
> I see your handiwork in the heavens. Ps 8:4
> What God says, God does. Ps 33:4

Feast of Thanksgiving

Thanksgiving is much more than a day. Thanksgiving is a spirit. If you believe that, anytime could be a time to make the line from Psalm 34 come alive, "Taste and see the goodness of the Lord."

Taste—relish that goodness within your very being, for you are the beloved, the one in whom God takes delight.

See—behold the goodness surrounding you:

> In nature preparing for winter,
>> In family, friends, passers-by,
>> In events that in the long haul, prove to be best
> for you.

When I was ill and in pain, I was aware that from the "good morning" tray to drawing the drapes at night, there always seemed to be one more need. Caring responses from those around me initiated in me a brand new awareness of being encircled by God's love. I'm sure you've had similar experiences.

Why not drink in, enjoy, and relish how the goodness of the Lord permeates life?

Reflection

To paraphrase Psalm 34, Bless the Lord at <u>all</u> times. Praise the Lord throughout your day. Let your whole being *glory* in the Lord because this *is* what it means to taste and see the goodness of the Lord.

You're in for a *feast* of *Thanksgiving*.

Pray the Psalms

I bring a gift of thanks, as I call on your name. Ps 116:17

Praise the Lord my heart! My whole life gives praise. Ps 146:2

The Christmas Season

The Advent and Christmas season has its own special vocabulary—words that are integral to the season. Beginning with *Jesus*—God's Word, made flesh, we remember that all Christmas words had their beginning because "the Word became flesh."

In Luke's gospel, we find *angels* singing, "Glory to God in the highest." *Carols* tell the story of that wondrous night when *shepherds* become very important people, and foreign *magi* enter the song. *Stars* lead, leap, and light. Everything speaks of *gift*-giving. Throughout the ages, Christmas words have been added. Bells, wreaths, Santa, candles and Christmas trees are just a few. But always, these words are rooted in the *Love* that found its way from heaven to earth.

Caryll Houselander, in her book, *The Reed of God*, says, "When Mary surrendered herself to God, there was indeed a miraculous New Heaven and New Earth." What did Mary do? Mary simply gathered all her daily experiences of the world about her to the Word growing within her.

Does that give you an idea for this Advent/Christmas season? Believe that the Word is growing within you, too. Believe that so firmly that you cannot help relating everything, literally *everything*, to this incredible reality.

Reflection

If we try each day to embody Christmas words—*joy, peace, love,* the miracle of that first Christmas could happen again, and when we begin to truly *live*—and give *life* to—these words, there will be *gifts* every day. In the words of Psalm 66, we could also say, "Lord God, I come to your house with gifts."

God remembered his sacred word...and brought forth his people...singing for joy (Ps 105:42-3).

Pray the Psalms

> May the Lord bless his people with peace. Ps 29:11
> I rejoice in your love each morning. Ps 59:17
> Let the hills ring out their joy. Ps 98:8

End Notes

For those serious about "Interior Remodeling," "Heart Work," "Getting to Know You, God," and growing awareness of "God Moments," and for those seeking a change of heart, here are additional Psalm lines and a few soul push-ups (reflective exercising). They will transform "A Nothing Day" and fill you with "Soul Music." In season and out, these guides will set you walking—even dancing—in the presence of the One who loves you unconditionally, extravagantly.

I. Getting to Know You, God

1. Strong the love embracing us.   Ps 117:2
2. Delight in God who satisfies your heart.   Ps 37:4
3. You are a God full of love.   Ps 86:15
4. What God says, God does.   Ps 33:4
5. You open wide your hand.   Ps 145:16
6. God stays near broken hearts.   Ps 34:19
7. Show me your wonderful love.   Ps 17:7
8. Alone the Maker of worlds!   Ps 136:4
9. Gracious God, you strengthen the weak.   Ps 68:11
10. Lord, you give from your goodness.   Ps 119:68

Know the God who created you.

1. Mend something broken like Jesus did.
2. Maybe, un-schedule something to make room for the Spirit.
3. Find ways to know people of a different culture.
4. Let someone know you care.
5. On whom can I lean—like a rock?

II. God Moments

1. See the wonders God does.	Ps 46:9
2. Show me a sign of your love.	Ps 86:17
3. Whoever seeks your help finds how lavish you are.	Ps 31:20
4. Teach us to make use of our days.	Ps 90:12
5. Lord, you show your care for us.	Ps 40:6
6. I wrap you in my mercy.	Ps 71:21
7. Turn to God, be bright with joy.	Ps 34:6
8. My God, I lean on you.	Ps 18:3
9. God you keep our spirits alive.	Ps 66:9
10. I deliver all who cling to me.	Ps 91:14

Discover how the Spirit energizes us in unbelievable ways.

1. Psalm 149 says, "God opens blind eyes." Ask. Believe.
2. Notice and praise God in the extraordinary variety of creation.
3. Don't give up, give in to the Spirit's enthusiasm.
4. Who needs a listening ear?
5. Remember who loves you, and be happy.

III. Heart Work

1. I, your God, choose the moment to set
   things right.   Ps 75:3
2. Your care lifts my spirit.   Ps 94:19
3. Creator God, reshape my heart.   Ps 51:12
4. I have wisdom you need to hear.   Ps 49:4
5. O God, welcome us with love.   Ps 79:8
6. Shower my life with your tenderness,
   Lord.   Ps 119:77
7. Attend to your heart.   Ps 4:5
8. I offer you a changed heart.   Ps 51:19
9. God's love is from all ages.   Ps 103:17
10. Lord, our God, the whole world tells
    the greatness of your name.   Ps 8:2

Create a new heart, a new spirit within you: God's promise.

1. Notice today's blessings and be grateful.
2. Follow your heart's promptings.
3. Say the "good word" that stops gossip.
4. Ask God's blessing on someone.
5. Remember the Giver of all good gifts.

IV. Interior Remodeling

1. This is the work of the Lord.   Ps 118:23
2. Inspire me to learn your wisdom.   Ps 119:73
3. You set my heart free.   Ps 119:32
4. Always look for the power of God.   Ps 105:4
5. You guide me along sure paths.   Ps 23:3
6. Lift me up, God.   Ps 69:30
7. All you touch comes alive.   Ps 65:12

8. Who can forget God's wonders?	Ps 111:4
9. The Lord is my Shepherd. I shall not want.	Ps 23:1
10. Be still. Wait for the Lord.	Ps 37:7

Look deeper into who you are.

1. Be generous with encouragement.
2. Who needs your forgiveness?
3. Find the beauty in others.
4. Try to open the circle of your love.
5. Pray for someone that you find difficult.

V. A Nothing Day

1. Enrich those you love.	Ps 17:14
2. Look for the presence of God.	Ps 105:4
3. God works wonders. Rejoice! Be glad!	Ps 126:3
4. Dry as thirsty land, I reach out for you.	Ps. 143:6
5. God turns the desert into flowing water.	Ps 107:35
6. Look for the face of God.	Ps 27:8
7. Bless the work we do. Ps	90:17
8. Lord, show me the right way.	Ps 143:8
9. You fill my life with riches.	Ps 103:5
10. I trust in God's word.	Ps 130:5

Turn "nothing" into a shimmering day with God.

1. Let God's power work through you.
2. Remember things aren't always what they seem—people, too.
3. Put some life where there is sameness.
4. Help someone feel how beautiful she/he is.

5. Try seeing with God's eyes

VI. Soul Music

1. I will sing to you, 0 Lord, sing your love.   Ps 101:1
2. Awake, my soul to song.   Ps 57:9
3. My whole life gives praise.   Ps 146:2
4. I will shout your praise.   Ps 51:17
5. My flesh sings its joy to the Living God.   Ps 84:3
6. I thank God in song.   Ps 28:7
7. Let my song give joy to God, who is a joy to me.   Ps 104:34
8. Play music to match your shout of joy.   Ps 33:3
9. Listen today to God's voice.   Ps 95:8
10. My strength, my song is the Lord.   Ps 118:14

Sing: To sing is to pray twice.

1. Try singing "Alleluia" to whatever happens today.
2. Hum a happy tune in your heart and sometimes, let others hear it.
3. "I'm sorry" is a beautiful sound.
4. Throughout the day be aware of the music around you.
5. As you retire, sing thanks for today's blessings.

VII. 'Tis The Season

1. Bless God who fills your life with richness   Ps 103:5
2. My cup is overflowing.   Ps 23:5
3. Now is the moment.   Ps 65:2
4. God, how fertile your genius!   Ps 104:24

5. All you touch comes alive.   Ps 65:12
6. You changed my sorrow into joy.   Ps 30:12
7. Strong the love embracing us.   Ps 117:2
8. Open my eyes to your beauty.   Ps 119:18
9. You fill the world with awe.   Ps 104: 1
10. Praise the God of lasting love.   Ps 106:1

Discover Jesus throughout the Church's liturgical seasons.

1. Try giving others another chance.
2. Give without expecting thanks.
3. "God so loved the world that he gave his only Son"; so, today, I will love…
4. How would joy change your life?
5. Do something beautiful. Do it joyfully.

About the Author

Regine Fanning, a Religious Sister of Mercy of the Americas, was a teacher for many years. She taught children in kindergarten through high school. She earned A Master of Arts from Mundelein College, A Master of Education from the University of Illinois and a Master of Applied Spirituality from Xavier University in San Francisco.

Sister found each level of teaching a joy. Her belief that each student held a gift to be opened presented a challenge, but then, as one of her published poems explained, "The Gift that I want to open is *Imagination*." Her class schedule could be described as *fresh* and *inviting*. Each level spent Friday afternoons creatively, and each listened to a story before heading home. Words being contagious, hopefully, her students caught on.

A published poet, Regine won first prize in a California State Poetry contest as well as recognition in several other contests. Her work has appeared in Penwood Review, California State Poetry Society Publications, The Oak, The Shepherd, The Mast, and The Thomas Merton Institute Collection.

Several of Regine's children's books have been published, the most recent, *Circles of Joy,* a book about the psalms *for* children not *about* children. In fact, *Circles of*

Joy includes inspiration for parents, grandparents, catechists, teachers and homeschoolers.

Eager to share the happiness and God hunger that the Psalms can bring, Regine formed a group to do "one good thing" that could not be kept secret. Each month the group made a small envelope-shaped note with a psalm line to deliver to patients at two local hospitals. The note was titled, "A Psalm in my Heart". Patients remarked that the particular lines were just what they needed—actual evidence of the Spirit's gifting. At the same time, the healing power confirmed Regine's long held belief in the mystery and power of the Psalms.

Building on her teaching experience, Regine ministered as a Children's Religious Instruction Coordinator (CCD Coordinator), and Rite of Christian Initiation for Adults (RCIA) retreat leader, Pastoral Associate and Spiritual Companion. Her teaching and ministries are the source and foundation for her poetry and prose.

As CCD Coordinator, she designed a training program for volunteer catechists and a children's program, featuring music as the universal language.

CCD ministry evolved into Pastoral Associate with opportunities to write a weekly parish scripture reflection, to lead adult seasonal scripture sessions and to initiate *Lovin' Links*, a parish prayer group for married couples.

Spirit Script originated in 1994 as a way to spiritually companion the homebound in the form of a monthly letter. Characteristic of the Spirit, it changed to fit the needs of participants and increased to five hundred mailings, sent to sixteen states. Gradually, readership included professionals who ministered at parishes, hospitals, schools and religious education groups.

Spirit Script in its present form flows from Regine's desire to offer a distinctive prayer resource that is current, encouraging and nourishing, but not heavy. It promises to stimulate the quest for deeper prayer resting on the experience of words, music, and wonder.

Interestingly, a professional evaluation of Regine's work style noted:

> "Your responses seem to indicate that you tend to spend your energies more in creating structures for and organizing ministries than in engaging one-to-one direct service. You are a developer of other people. In addition, your capacity for empathy and your ability to listen to people is a way in which you often give yourself."

Sister Regine's comment was:

> "After many years, people, places and especially God's grace *I'm becoming myself.*"Ximaxim qui cum dit quae pra expere consequi destis suntoribeat.

www.ingramcontent.com/pod-product-compliance
Lightning Source LLC
Chambersburg PA
CBHW071144160426
43196CB00011B/2011